RENEWAL

LEADING DIRECT SELLING TURNAROUNDS

BRETT A. BLAKE

Author of
Private Equity Investing in Direct Selling:
Identifying Risks & Rewards

RENEWAL: Leading Direct Selling Turnarounds
© 2020 Brett A. Blake. All rights reserved.

ISBN-13: 978-1-7333568-2-4

No part of this publication may be reproduced or transmitted in any form or by any means, mechanical or electronic, including photocopying and recording, or by any information storage and retrieval system, without permission in writing from author or publisher (except by a reviewer, who may quote brief passages and/or show brief video clips in a review).

CONTENTS

Introduction: Going South—*Learning the Leadership Lessons of Renewal*	v
Chapter 1: Defying Gravity—*An Industry with a Clear Pattern*	11
Chapter 2: A Tale of Two Tails—*Failure to Renewal vs. Failure to Renew*	23
Chapter 3: Seeing Around Corners—*Anticipating Slower Growth or Sales Declines*	33
Chapter 4: The Renewal C.H.I.S.E.L.—*Six Variables Every Renewal Plan Should Include*	45
Chapter 5: Cash—*The Oxygen of Your Business*	51
Chapter 6: Hope—*Fuel for the Field*	79
Chapter 7: Innovation—*Most Likely Your Key to Renewal*	97
Chapter 8: System Innovation—*The Most Overlooked Renewal Tool*	105
Chapter 9: Product Innovation—*Evolutionary or Revolutionary?*	123
Chapter 10: Compensation Innovation—*Rewarding Growth with the Right Incentives*	137
Chapter 11: Simplify—*Removing Layers to Discover the Core*	149
Chapter 12: Expanding to New Markets—*Finding New Customers in New Places*	161
Chapter 13: Expanding to New Domestic Markets —*No Passports Required*	165
Chapter 14: Expanding to International Markets —*Finding the Majority of Today's Sales*	173
Chapter 15: Leading During Tough Times—*Being Present and Positive*	187
Chapter 16: Beyond Your C.H.I.S.E.L.—*Other Considerations That Impact Pace*	197
Chapter 17: When You Fail to Renew—*Other Options When Growth Doesn't Happen*	205
Chapter 18: The Direct Selling Fraternity—*Turning to Help from Other Direct Sellers*	215
Acknowledgments	221
About the Author	225

BRETT A. BLAKE

INTRODUCTION: GOING SOUTH—
Learning the Leadership Lessons of Renewal

> "Leadership and learning are indispensable to each other."
>
> — JOHN F. KENNEDY

N

It wasn't my first international trip, but it was my first time flying international first class and the first time I had been excited about flying United Airlines (I was a Delta frequent flyer). The experience was far superior to any flight I had taken in my previous 33 years and I was impressed, not with the drinks (I don't drink) and not with the food (it was almost midnight and I wasn't hungry) but with the lay-flat beds, thick blanket and personal pillow I was issued. My sleep was sound, the 14-hour flight was short, and I landed in Sydney in time to make it to my new office for my first day.

Despite the restful flight, jet lag got the best of me when I tried to make a left-hand turn in downtown Sydney and suddenly found myself in a very awkward situation. All of the parked cars and those coming my way seemed to be heading the wrong direction. I was sure they had all made a mistake until my mind broke through the fog and I realized I was on the wrong side of the road and going the wrong way on a one-way street. I had no choice but to back up into the busy intersection, regain my bearings and continue to my hotel—this time on the left side of the road and going with the flow of traffic.

I had been sent to Australia for an indefinite period of time to address an urgent business crisis for our direct selling company and to right-size a division that was hemorrhaging cash and had seen sales drop from nearly $50 million to just $25 million. The crisis resulted in three lawyers (one hired by the previous general manager, one hired by the current general manager and the last by our then-marketing manager).

After a shower I drove to the office to interview the current management and to dive into the economics of the subsidiary. My interviews didn't lead to new discoveries but gave me a firsthand account of what I had been told before. The previous general manager had been let go on account of the free-fall in sales and the lack of a plan to address the decline. His predecessor had been on the job for less than a month when a senior manager accused him of sexual harassment and therefore needed to be replaced. All of that was widely known, but what was not clear until these interviews was the fact that the marketing manager was not prepared or capable of making a meaningful contribution to the company's turnaround.

Just before retiring for bed that first night in Sydney, I called the home office in the United States to inform them that I had arrived and concluded that we had to fire the marketing manager as well.

Within the week, I had created and executed a plan to bring the employee base in-line with current sales, but what I thought would be the end of crisis management mode was only the beginning. By the end of the first month we would face three additional crises. The first was a story aired by the Australian Broadcasting Corporation (ABC) about a man who had called himself a doctor but had no medical credentials. In the B-roll or background footage of that news story they ran images of our company's products, clearly leading viewers to believe this man was associated with us. He wasn't. The second was the news that the new skincare line we were set to launch the following month at a series of live events had sold out in the U.S. We would not be able to have product for our markets (Australia and New Zealand) for three to six months. And finally, as if those other issues weren't bad enough, we received a letter threatening a lawsuit over our products.

Over the next six months we would resolve all legal matters for less than $10K, we would demand and receive an on-air and written apology from ABC, and we would see steady growth in sales from month two and beyond. I left the country within six months having hired a new general manager of subsidiaries that were profitable and growing.

This experience would be the beginning of a career working with companies and subsidiaries in need of Renewal. While I can't claim a 100% success rate, I'm proud of the condition I left each of the companies in. One of them should not have survived but did. Another found a large corporate buyer. Another that had declined more than 40% before my arrival had rebounded to within 1% of the previous year's sales by the time I left, and two achieved long-term growth leading to total annual sales of more than $1 billion each.

As is the case in many experiences in life, I've learned critical lessons in each of the above circumstances. In fact, I probably learned more from the not so successful experiences than from those that were true turnarounds. But it didn't occur to me that my experience would be valuable to others until I had stepped away from the day-to-day work. It took time away from an operating role and the chance to connect with CEOs and executives running companies in need of *Renewal* before all of the lessons learned came together in a system that I believe can be followed by any direct selling company. In fact, I didn't realize how common the need for Renewal was until I completed the research necessary to record and graph the sales of dozens of direct selling companies for another book I wrote.[1] During that research I came to understand that every direct selling company has gone through a period of Renewal. Even the most successful have had at least one period of declining sales. The oldest and most successful have experienced multiple periods of Renewal.

While the great companies have experienced decline and found a way to renew growth, there are plenty of examples of companies that

---

[1] *Private Equity Investing in Direct Selling: Identifying Risks and Rewards*

have experienced declines and never returned to growth... or even worse, have continued to decline—some until they were claimed by bankruptcy, sold to one of the firms creating conglomerates from the remnants of failed or failing companies, changed channels or closed their doors. We lament the stars of yesteryear that are gone now, like Longaberger[2], and those that have become a much smaller version of their past selves, like Pampered Chef and Creative Memories.

Renewal: Leading Direct Selling Turnarounds presents an inventory of the variables executives should include in their turnaround plan. I wrote this book to help you focus on the things that will increase your chances of stopping a decline and renewing growth in your company. The review of these variables will not be granular enough to provide detailed solutions for every company, but will offer specific areas of focus and examples of work done by others. My goal is to provide as much guidance as possible to help you lead your company during a downturn in sales and find your way back to renewed growth.

Finally, while this book has been written primarily for company executives and CEOs, I have included a section in several chapters with specific advice to field leaders. I do believe that a company is more likely to experience Renewal more quickly if field leaders go through the experience with their eyes wide open and understand their role in leading during challenging times.

This book offers a set of variables to include in your turnaround plan, but I'm confident that the most important ingredient to your future success will be your leadership (that and a little bit of luck). Your commitment to reading and understanding "what you should do" is a critical first step and is evidence that you have the humility to admit that the things you've been doing during your period of growth (or Hyper-Growth) won't be the answer to *renewing* growth. In the end, applying your learning and leading with courage will be the enabling factors in your company's success.

Let's get started.

---

[2] Longaberger did announce an attempt to relaunch starting with QVC just as we were preparing to publish the first edition of this book.

BRETT A. BLAKE

CHAPTER 1: DEFYING GRAVITY—
An Industry with a Clear Pattern

> "There is no such thing as a company that grows forever without eventually hitting the wall, or at least slowing down to go over a speed bump."
>
> — RON ASHKENAS, *HARVARD BUSINESS REVIEW*

By the time I decided to leave Beachbody so I could move closer to my mom who was battling life-threatening cancer, I was certain I knew how to be successful in direct selling. I had started my career at Melaleuca and rode their wave from just above $20 million in sales to $105 million and left just after we reached $210 million. I joined USANA during a period of decline and after the board gave me the chance to craft and implement a strategy, the company began to grow again (and has seen steady growth every year for more than 15 years). When I arrived at Beachbody, its direct selling division—Team Beachbody—was in decline. It had grown to approximately $50 million on the back of an infomercial referral program, but when the economics of their model forced them to pull the plug on that program, the division's sales dropped. When I arrived in January of 2010, Team Beachbody was producing just a bit more than $3 million a month and several top leaders were considering "full-time jobs." As GM of that division, I was proud of the fact that we would close 2013 at just under $400 million in sales.

I'll be the first to admit that I had very little to do with the success of these three companies, but having lived and breathed each experience, I was fairly certain I understood how to grow and regrow network marketing companies. However, I was about to learn of the truth of behavioral scientist Daniel Kahneman's conclusion that "declarations of high confidence mainly tell you that an individual has constructed a coherent story in his mind, not necessarily that the story is true." [3]

I left an operating role at Beachbody and joined their Board of Directors and took a job as the CEO of a very small party-plan company called Jewel Kade. I accepted the job in part because it allowed me to move close to my mom, in part because it allowed me to avoid competing with Beachbody, and also because I recognized that party-plan companies tend to hit a wall as they grow. My confidence (or arrogance) led me to conclude that I could actually help solve that problem, not only at Jewel Kade but for other party-plan companies as well.

During the next several years, first at Jewel Kade and then at Origami Owl, I would learn that applying tactics with success at one company didn't always lead to success at another. I recognized how easy it is to exaggerate our own importance—or even the importance of knowledge and skill—and to underestimate the role of luck and chance.

While I'm extraordinarily proud of the work we did and the outcomes at both Jewel Kade (sold to Thirty-One Gifts) and Origami Owl (returned to the owners with a bright future today), neither of those companies has experienced the same record of sales growth I've seen at other companies.

The learning and humility gained at both of these party-plan companies and a short tenure at AdvoCare helped me to reflect on the key variables a CEO must focus on when presented with a decline in their business. When asked to share my ideas on this subject with the executive team of a large company experiencing its first decline, I was frankly surprised by their positive response which encouraged me to put my learning in a book with the hope that others may be helped by my successes and failures.

---

[3] Daniel Kahneman, *Thinking, Fast and Slow* (New York: Farrar, Straus & Giroux), 2013.

I don't believe that every company can be saved. I don't believe that great leadership is the only key to turning sales around. Companies are dynamic and face millions of outside influences that can impact success or failure. Competition, market trends, social media algorithms, distributor claims, supply chain integrities and even weather can impact a company's results. As Kahneman puts it:

> *Narrative fallacies arise inevitably from our continuous attempt to make sense of the world. The explanatory stories that people find compelling are simple; are concrete rather than abstract; assign a larger role to talent, stupidity, and intentions than to luck; and focus on a few striking events that happened rather than on the countless events that failed to happen. Any recent salient event is a candidate to become the kernel of a causal narrative. Taleb suggests that we humans constantly fool ourselves by constructing flimsy accounts of the past and believing they are true.* [4]

"Countless events" can contribute to success or failure, but I believe that failure is certain if a company's leadership doesn't understand and address key variables during a downturn. The variables I will introduce to you in this book are not an elixir, but I do believe that ignoring them will guarantee failure. The "C.H.I.S.E.L." variables I describe later in this book will provide leaders like you (both corporate and field) the essential building blocks that should guide attention and planning as you respond to the inevitable downturn that will come to your business.

Yes, I said "inevitable downturn."

YOUR BUSINESS WILL EXPERIENCE NO GROWTH, SLOW GROWTH AND A DECLINE

Believe it or not, your company is not destined to continuous and unencumbered growth. At least among direct selling companies, history tells a narrative of three to five years of Hyper-Growth followed

[4] Ibid.

by a few years of no growth or decline. How the company and its field leaders respond to the period of decline will determine whether it will continue or be replaced with renewed growth.

To illustrate my point, I have included a visual chart showing six direct selling companies that went through rapid growth, decline and found renewed growth. It's true that most of these companies are public (it's difficult to get reliable information on private companies that can be published), but my experience tells me that every private company that undergoes similar Hyper-Growth will also go through a time of retraction.

SCENTSY

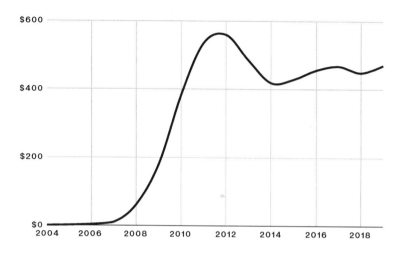

THIRTY-ONE GIFTS

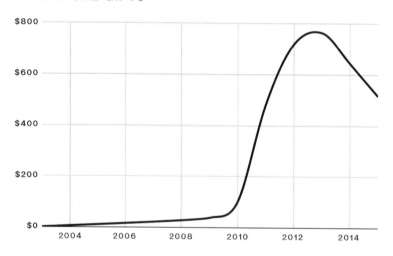

NU SKIN

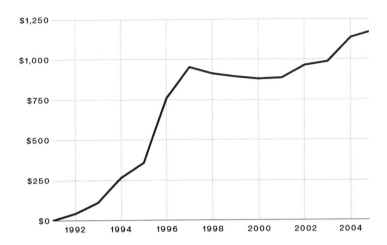

USANA HEALTH SCIENCES

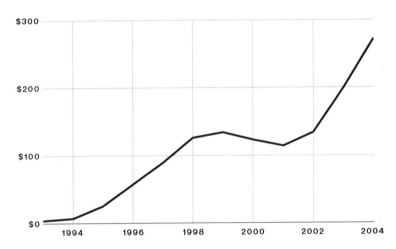

ARBONNE INTERNATIONAL

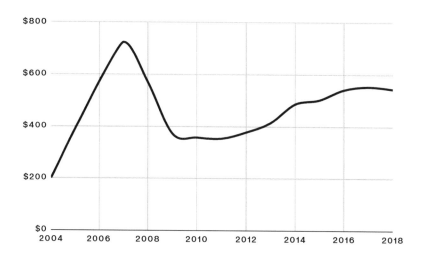

NATURA

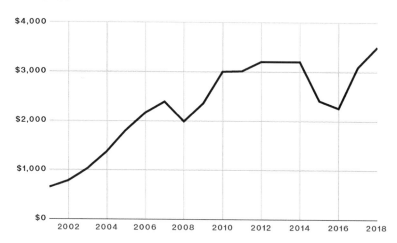

All of these examples show companies that were able to regain traction, and a few had sustainable sales for many years after their initial decline. The data to which I've had access leads me to believe that there is something about direct selling companies that makes it historically impossible to sustain rapid growth in the early years without experiencing a flattening or decline later.

Why do direct sales companies fail to sustain growth year after year? One of the theories for the decline after years of strong growth is that these companies' sales outpace the development of field leaders to support the number of distributors recruited. Because of the channel's dependence on volunteer sales and organically acquired field leadership, often revenues tend to overtake a company's ability to grow the field leadership. Author Eric Worre teaches that most companies can only grow leadership at a rate of 10% per year, and sales growth above that rate forewarns future declines. In an interview I had with LifeVantage CEO Darren Jensen, he described this challenge:

> *Too many investors are attracted by a company in the "pop phase" not knowing that as a rule of thumb it will only run for eighteen months or so, and then there's a one hundred percent probability that the company will either implode or that they will go through a glide or flat phase. They will see a flattening of the business or a slow downward glide while the underlying distributor leadership base catches up with the revenue.*

Subscribers to Worre's leadership sustainability theory argue that sales will continue to decline or remain flat until they reach a level the field leaders can manage—either via declining sales or increasing leadership.

"The key is to understand that a slowing, flattening and often a downward glide in sales is a predicable reaction to significant sales growth," Jensen added.

The purpose of this book is not to diagnose the cause or to suggest preventative action. I don't pretend to have a valid theory for either. Instead, the goal of this book is to prepare direct selling executives and field leaders for a reversal, to help them recognize the problem early, and to give them a tool kit for responding and renewing their company's growth.

Knowing that no direct selling company will have continuous uninterrupted sales growth should be both frightening and comforting to executives. It should leave you with a sobering expectation that the work in front of you may not always be about playing catch-up and may temper your enthusiasm for making capital investments before the inevitable correction. It should also help those of you who have experienced a spike followed by a fall to forgive yourselves and not take the results so personally. A downward slide is not always a sign of poor leadership. Corrections happen, but whether they prove to be little bumps in the road or a continuously declining experience for your company can be influenced by the decisions you make and your ability to focus on all the right things.

My goal is to equip you to make all the right decisions by helping you see the spectrum of variables that need your attention during a time of Renewal. But before I introduce you to the "C.H.I.S.E.L." variables, I want to share two true tales of companies that experienced declining sales and the dramatic difference in the end result for each.

RENEWAL

CHAPTER 2: A TALE OF TWO TAILS—
Failure to Renewal vs. Failure to Renew

"The illusion that one has understood the past feeds the further illusion that one can predict and control the future. These illusions are comforting. They reduce the anxiety that we would experience if we allowed ourselves to fully acknowledge the uncertainties of existence. We all have a need for the reassuring message that actions have appropriate consequences, and that success will reward wisdom and courage. Many business books are tailor-made to satisfy this need."

— DANIEL KAHNEMAN, *THINKING, FAST AND SLOW*

N

Dave Longaberger and Mark Hughes both founded and led a direct selling company to national prominence during their lifetime. Both had struggled in school. Mark dropped out in the 9th grade before being compelled to return to a school for troubled students. Dave stuck with it but was held back in the first grade, forced to repeat 5th grade twice, and didn't graduate from high school until he was 21. Both Dave and Mark were beloved by the distributors in the companies they founded. They died about one year apart—Mark at age 44 and Dave at age 64.

While Dave and Mark had many things in common, their reputations as CEOs of the companies they founded were actually vastly different. Dave came from a large family in the Midwest and built a company selling baskets he had learned to build from his father and grandfather. Mark grew up an only child with a single mother near Los Angeles and his company was built to sell weight loss supplements. While both companies used the direct selling channel, each sold with its own twist on compensating and selling (party-plan vs. network marketing). Dave built a "family" company from a small town in Southeast Ohio while Mark was a solo entrepreneur who built a company that flaunted the stereotypical Hollywood lifestyle.

Dave was the talk at all direct selling association meetings and was a darling of the government and media in Ohio. As his company grew, he hired more and more homegrown employees and built a corporate headquarters in the shape of a basket (the company's core product line) with its own public golf course. To the outside world, Dave's basket company, Longaberger, was built to last. It employed no "get rich quick" selling tactics and focused on rewarding product sales to end consumers. Not only that, but Dave and his company were model citizens.

Mark's company, Herbalife, couldn't have been more different. No one would accuse Mark of building a family company, in part because Mark had no family to build his company with or around, and in part because he displayed an openly rebellious streak. Herbalife faced actions from the Federal Drug Administration, the California State Attorney General, the California State Department of Health, the Department of Justice of Canada, two Herbalife distributors and company shareholders. Mark took on Congress with a brashness rarely seen in those hallowed halls when the federal government made moves to regulate nutritional supplements. The *LA Times* reported that "a U.S. Senate subcommittee called Hughes before a hearing in May. Referring to a panel of nutrition experts who had criticized Herbalife in testimony the previous day, he asked the senators, 'If they're such experts in weight loss, why were they so fat?'" [5]

Herbalife grew quickly and profitably in its first few years, but when it received so much negative press from government probes, it began to retract. Even when sales began to grow again in the 1990s, many believed that the company was a house of cards that someday would implode and self-destruct.

And then tragedy struck both companies. Dave Longaberger was diagnosed with kidney cancer and died less than a year later on March 17, 1999. Mark Hughes had no time to prepare. On May 20, 2000 he was found dead in his Malibu beach house of an apparent accidental overdose. [6]

---

[5] https://www.latimes.com/archives/la-xpm-2000-may-22-me-32795-story.html accessed August 1, 2019.
[6] https://web.archive.org/web/20130313003715/http://articles.cnn.com/2000-06-17/us/hughes.death_1_accidental-overdose-final-autopsy-results-malibu-mansion?_s=PM%3AUS, accessed November 5, 2019.

Two direct selling founders, dead. Two successful companies with sales around one billion dollars, both starting over without their enthusiastic founders.

In the immediate aftermath of the founders' deaths, Longaberger's and Herbalife's sales reacted differently. Herbalife began a slow decline while Longaberger's sales continued to grow reaching a billion dollars in annual sales the year of Dave's death. Had experts been told at the time that one of these companies would become one of the world's largest direct sellers and the other would fail, most would have predicted Longaberger as the winner and Herbalife the loser. That prediction wouldn't have been more wrong.

Twenty years later, we are left to contemplate two very different results. Anyone with access to Google or a cursory knowledge of today's direct selling companies will know that Longaberger and Herbalife defied the public opinion of their time. Herbalife has grown to become a top five direct selling company in sales, and has created billions of dollars of value for public shareholders. On the opposite tail of our tale, Longaberger is gone. After Dave's death, Longaberger experienced a sudden surge of sales and then slowly and steadily declined until it was sold to a company that became insolvent. The basket shaped headquarters stands in disrepair—a sad symbol of what might have been.

The stories of these two companies represent extreme examples of what is possible when direct selling companies face adversity. A company's history isn't a good predictor of its future. These examples prove the truth of the first half of Winston Churchill's famous maxim: "Success is not final" and the fallacy of the second half: "Failure is not fatal." Failure can, in fact, be fatal. Herbalife found a way to turn what many believed was certain failure into Renewal, then growth and long-term success. Longaberger rode a wave of short-term success, but when the wave subsided management failed to take the necessary steps to renew their opportunity and suffered the complete loss of their utopia-like company.

Before I introduce you to the six variables CEOs should manage in their effort to find Renewal and offer suggestions to field leaders who have their own businesses to protect and grow, I think it would be helpful to dig a little deeper into the tales of these two companies to try and understand what's possible on both ends of the proverbial tail. I think it is also helpful to be clear that I'm not offering a formula that is a panacea. Direct selling businesses are complex with their web of human relationships and not all turnaround efforts will succeed. I have learned from personal experience that previous success doesn't always guarantee future success. However, I do believe that failure will be certain if leaders (1) don't understand the breadth of variables that must be managed, and (2) allow one or more of the variables to take its course without management's attention.

HERBALIFE: FROM FAILURE TO RENEWAL

Mark Hughes founded Herbalife selling weight loss products from the trunk of his car in 1980. By 1985, *Inc.* magazine recognized Herbalife as one of the fastest growing companies in America and sales grew from just $386 thousand to $423 million in its first five years.[7] That same year, the company was sued by the California State Attorney General's office and sales plummeted, forcing the company to lay off 800 employees in May of 1985.[8] As the chart shows, the company's sales continued to fall for the next few years. Despite the poor sales performance, Hughes led the company through a public offering and began expanding internationally, somehow finding a way to renew growth through the 1990s.

In 2000, when Mark Hughes died, the company had already begun to decline in sales and his death rattled public markets and field leaders. It was struggling as a public company, and the short-term expectation was for it to continue the downward sales trajectory.

After a few years of decline, in 2002, the company was purchased

---

[7] https://www.inc.com/magazine/19851201/8371.html, accessed November 5, 2019.
[8] https://www.latimes.com/archives/la-xpm-1985-05-29-fi-7634-story.html, accessed November 5, 2019.

and taken private by private equity investors J.H. Whitney & Company and Golden Gate Capital. The new owners discontinued controversial products and ingredients and brought in former Walt Disney executive Michael O. Johnson as CEO. These efforts reassured distributors and the company experienced a second Renewal and growth that was sustained for many years. This time the downturn was significant but short-lived, and Renewal occurred after just two years of decline.

HERBALIFE SALES CHART

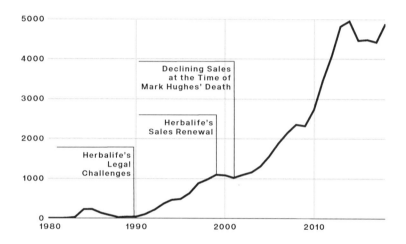

LONGABERGER'S FAILURE TO RENEW

The tale of Longaberger includes far fewer financial reports, but as the chart shows, the company's surge to a billion the year of Dave's death did not last. Instead, that peak was followed by a long and steady decline resulting in the absolute failure of the company in 2018.

Unlike Mark Hughes, Dave Longaberger had some warning before his death. He brought in outside management and gave his daughter Tami (who would become the company's CEO after his death) more and more responsibility. Unfortunately, this preparation did little to improve the outcome for Longaberger. Those close to the company attribute its decline to a changing market for baskets, online markets like eBay that destroyed the collector's club built around their iconic baskets, and failed attempts to add product lines that weren't complementary but rather non-complementary, like jewelry.

When pushed to identify "the most significant" variable that led to Longaberger's eventual demise, former executives I interviewed agreed that a change in the compensation plan killed the field's enthusiasm and destroyed the long-standing trust and relationship that Dave had built between the company and its field leaders. Those interviewed said that it wasn't so much the changed compensation plan that destroyed the company but the way it was changed and the message it sent.

As sales declined, Longaberger's management became increasingly concerned that the compensation plan was rewarding top leaders but not motivating new distributors. Instead of engaging the whole management team in finding a solution to their concerns, then-CEO Tami Longaberger created a compensation plan with the help of outside consultants and told her team that she had decided to make a change. Company management learned of the plan just before it was announced to the field. When the changes were announced, field leaders were devastated and saw their compensation fall more than 30% immediately. Many top leaders were forced to return to part-time and full-time jobs. These demoralized leaders found it difficult to defend the changes and many lost their enthusiasm for selling and leading their teams.

Dave had always been known for bringing top leaders into the company, giving them a problem and saying to them "find a solution for us." Top leaders loved Dave and bought into the solutions they created and, unlike most companies, Longaberger had steady year-over-year growth with no need to figure out how to renew. After his death, field leaders wanted to support Tami, but her style was not Dave's style. By the time the new compensation plan was introduced, the top leaders were essentially estranged from the company they helped build.

Longaberger brought in many management team members, hired

consultants and eventually was "forced" to first announce that they would source pottery and other products from China (a HUGE departure from what had been a proud "Made in America" message since its founding) and then would sell 51.7% of the company to JRJR Networks.

JRJR Networks, formerly CVSL, Inc., was an undercapitalized public company that tried to create shareholder value by serving as a collector of essentially failed or failing direct selling companies. The company's end occurred simultaneously with Longaberger's announced closing and after JRJR Networks' stock had been suspended by the New York Stock Exchange and the delisting process had begun.[9]

LONGABERGER'S SALES CHART

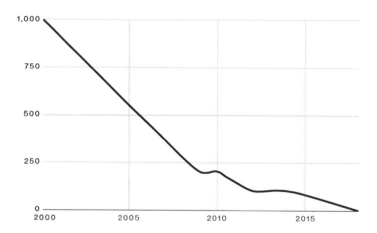

LESSONS LEARNED

I chose to include the stories of these two companies to remind you of the potential—both good and bad—for a company that begins to experience a decline. Herbalife and Longaberger are not alone at their respective tail ends of this tale of two companies. There are several examples of companies that have experienced signs of failure yet found a way to renew growth, as well as several examples of companies with continued decline and others that have experienced complete failure.

---

[9] https://www.dispatch.com/business/20180504/longaberger-story-coming-to-end, accessed September 12, 2019.

Momentum matters in direct selling, especially when it comes to recruiting others to connect their hopes and dreams to your company's products and opportunity, but momentum can be changed. Direct selling executives should be clear that momentum in either direction is not permanent. No company has experienced never-ending growth and no company has to experience perpetual decline. Leadership matters and company executives can make a difference in impacting both sides of momentum. Our focus in the coming chapters will be to provide direct selling leaders a set of variables that must be considered and proactively managed as part of their company's plan for Renewal. Those companies still in growth will also benefit from a study of these variables by learning what NOT to do and how to avoid making changes that needlessly stall your company's growth.

Let's begin by making sure you're keeping your eye on the Key Performance Indicators (KPIs) that will forewarn sales declines, and then introduce you to the variables that must be part of your Renewal plan.

CHAPTER 3: SEEING AROUND CORNERS—
Anticipating Slower Growth or Sales Declines

"It's not that we can predict bubbles—if we could, we would be rich. But we can certainly have a bubble warning system."

— RICHARD THAYER, AMERICAN ECONOMIST

N

At 7:02 a.m. December 7, 1941, volunteer George Elliott was practicing with new radar equipment that had been set up recently on the Opana, a knoll in the foothills of Oahu, Hawaii, when he detected incoming aircraft. The equipment that was installed as a warning system to help protect Pearl Harbor worked just as it should. Unfortunately, they were not able to warn the fleet at Pearl Harbor because when Elliott and his working companion, Joseph Lockard, called in to report what they saw to their superior, Lt. Kermit Tyler, Tyler "reasoned that the radar blip was a flight of Army B-17 bombers due in that morning. Lt. Tyler instructed the Opana Radar operations to disregard the information and not to worry about it."[10]

At 7:53 a.m., the first of two waves of Japanese aircraft attacked Pearl Harbor. Elliott and Lockard had closed up the radar center after being reassured that what they had seen were American aircraft, and they didn't find out what they had missed until after breakfast that morning. That morning "2,403 Americans were killed and 1,143 were wounded. Eighteen ships were sunk or run aground, including five battleships"[11] in a Japanese attack on Pearl Harbor.

I'm surprised how often direct selling companies have similar—though fortunately not fatal—experiences when they see signs that

---

[10] https://npgallery.nps.gov/NRHP/GetAsset/NHLS/91001379_text, accessed August 10, 2019.
[11] https://en.wikipedia.org/wiki/Attack_on_Pearl_Harbor accessed August 10, 2019.

should sound an alarm for their company. Instead of heeding the warnings and taking the appropriate actions, too many companies ignore or brush aside the data with a false confidence that they are signs that need not be responded to. In this chapter, we will provide a reminder to executives—especially those running companies that have seen three to five years of exceptional growth—that they should be on the lookout and ready to respond to early warning signs that the direction of their sales is about to change.

WHAT GOES UP...

Those who have studied the direct selling industry will recognize that there is a preponderance of evidence proving that direct selling companies do not continue to grow at double-digit rates forever. However, during times of double-digit growth, it's easy to ignore the evidence and perhaps even believe that you have stumbled upon something no other company before you has figured out: how to grow forever. To be fair, even rational executives who understand that their growth won't last forever sometimes are so consumed with managing their company's meteoric growth that they don't have the bandwidth to consider the possibility that their growth may someday slow and/or decline.

I suspect that if I had the opportunity to interview every executive whose company has seen sales slow and decline, they'd say they would have paid millions to have received advanced warning that their momentum was about to change. Yet, the experience of nearly every company in the industry would lead any objective thinker to conclude that sales growth never continues uninterrupted, and therefore every company should have an advanced warning system in place to help them see around the proverbial corner.

Waiting until sales start to slow or decline is too late. Companies need to be prepared to respond *before* they actually see the enemy overhead.

BUSINESS LIFECYCLE STAGES

Before we introduce you to an advanced warning system of sorts, let's first remind you of business lifecycle theory and define the stages of a company's life. Several individuals and institutions have their own version of the stages of a company, but I have chosen to define my own stages of a direct selling company and have based my model on a non-direct selling theory taught by The Corporate Finance Institute.[12] I believe understanding that all companies are susceptible to common lifecycle stages will help you to be less defensive about your company's transition from one stage to the next, and perhaps leave you more open to preparing for each stage so that you can make the necessary changes to extend your company's life and ensure *Renewal* rather than long-term decline.

I believe that direct selling companies experience the following lifecycle stages:

- Launch
- Hyper-Growth
- Growth by Promotion
- Shake-Out
- Decline or Renewal

STAGES IN THE LIFECYCLE OF A DIRECT SELLING COMPANY

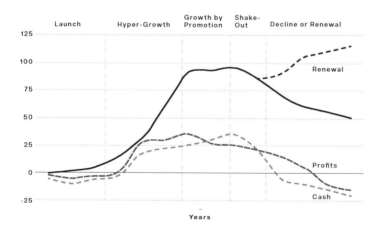

LIFECYCLE STAGE 1: LAUNCH

During the Launch stage, a company is figuring out its product, marketing, field compensation and selling systems. The Launch phase is marked by losses in both profits and cash as companies often use investor dollars or debt to fund operations. In direct selling, the Launch phase can be months or years depending on how long it takes to figure out selling systems that work and to recruit field leaders who are capable of exploiting those selling systems to grow the company.

LIFECYCLE STAGE 2: HYPER-GROWTH

Hyper-Growth quickly puts companies in the black with growing profits and plenty of cash, though not cash available for distribution. During this phase, cash generated by the business is often consumed almost entirely by needed capital investment and inventory purchases to keep up with the growth. The chart shows a positive cash flow, but a few companies experience so much growth that they are unable to fund growth from operating cash and are required to borrow to keep up. Nevertheless, their growth is so compelling that they rarely have difficulty in finding vendors (if not lenders) to help meet their need for cash. In other words, cash, whether from operations or from willing investors, is available and deployed quickly.

LIFECYCLE STAGE 3: GROWTH BY PROMOTION

During the Growth by Promotion stage, the company continues to grow, but that growth requires much more effort and expense. Companies get more aggressive with promotions, increase the number and frequency of product launches, and spend more and more on promotions to continue to grow. The pace of growth peaks during this stage before beginning to slow.

Because the company's growth no longer requires significant investment in infrastructure and inventory, companies in the Growth by Promotion stage have more cash available for distributions than at any previous stage. Founders often take large distributions and some

[12] https://corporatefinanceinstitute.com/resources/knowledge/finance/business-life-cycle/, accessed November 5, 2019.

founders cash-out in partnership with a private equity partner. Cash is plentiful, but profits and margins are declining on a relative basis as sales growth is driven by margin constraining promotions and/or new product introductions.

There are a number of common mistakes made during the Growth by Promotion stage. The combination of cash available for distribution and continued sales often mask this stage and many founders do not recognize that they have entered a new stage of growth that should cause them to save cash and begin retooling their strategies. Instead, too many owners unwittingly allow their company to continue to make decisions that constrain cash and make things difficult in future stages. Often companies will:

- **Continue to hire** and watch as the field becomes overwhelmed by the abundance of programs and initiatives designed by the "professional" teams built up to support the now much larger company.
- **Build or buy real estate.** In an effort to keep up with growth, companies often make long-term lease commitments or acquire real estate. Often these real estate commitments become painful consumers of much needed cash during later phases, and companies would be wise to delay long-term real estate decisions until they have safely found their way through their first real decline in sales.
- **Broaden their product line** in an effort to provide their field with more to sell or more to buy. Often the revenue per SKU begins to decline sharply indicating that these new products are not as lucrative. Companies quickly learn that more products mean more cash consumed by inventory and less available to fund needed investments to reverse future declines.

As the lifecycle chart illustrates, profits peak just as the company moves from the Hyper-Growth stage to the Growth by Promotion stage but interestingly enough, cash doesn't peak until late in the

Growth by Promotion stage and often not until the company's sales are already headed toward decline. Thus, using profits and cash flow as key indicators to warn of trouble ahead will leave executives responding too late.

LIFECYCLE STAGE 4: SHAKE-OUT

The Shake-Out stage is characterized by declining sales. During this phase, sales growth has not simply slowed, but sales are actually in decline. Often the first signs of a sales decline are attributed to seasonal slowing or a poor product launch. Missing the signs of decline can be costly because during the Shake-Out stage a company's cash position can change dramatically, often moving from peak cash production to a cash crisis within months.

First-time executives will often be surprised by how quickly their company changes from being a cash machine to a cash starved enterprise. This surprise is often brought on because the company has never had declining sales and all of the forecasts (even during the decline) continue to model optimism and the company is actually operating under a plan that predicts sales growth. When pushed to re-forecast the future based on current trends only (with no optimism built in to the model), management can quickly see that failing to cut costs immediately will leave them desperate for cash for future operations.

I have labeled this phase the "Shake-Out" stage because it is during this time when a company will make the decisions and adaptations that will eventually lead them either toward Renewal and additional growth, or decline—too often rapid decline.

LIFECYCLE STAGE 5: DECLINE OR RENEWAL

During the Decline or Renewal stage the company either makes necessary changes to improve topline sales or they see cash move into negative territory and run out of options. The model above shows a dotted line for Renewal, but the profit and cash lines only show the results of continued decline.

Because direct selling is often overlooked by capital providers,[13] often it is impossible for a direct selling company to survive a negative cash position (conversely tech companies like Amazon and Lendio have years of negative cash from operations but easily close the gap with capital from debt and equity investors).

Though not charted, those companies that are attentive to the variables I will introduce in the chapters to follow will make significant operating improvements to their business. Therefore, when they are able to renew growth in topline sales, both their profit and cash positions rebound dramatically. Unless they enter Hyper-Growth again, the company returns to be a very healthy cash producer.

ADVANCED WARNING SYSTEMS

After ten years in business and a period of Hyper-Growth, Thirty-One Gifts found themselves knocking on the door of $800 million in sales with everyone expecting growth to continue. Suddenly and unexpectedly the business changed, and the company dropped from a peak of $763 million to $512 million in just two years. In an article published by *The Columbus Dispatch* in 2017, CEO Cindy Monroe is quoted as saying, "We were growing so fast we didn't necessarily see it coming... We weren't sure it was a bump or new trend."[14]

Cindy Monroe is one of the best leaders I've met, and she has since led Thirty-One Gifts to an impressive recovery. I use her as an example, because I want to make the point that even great leaders can miss important cues if they aren't looking for them or don't know what to look for. Monroe's surprise is typical of many of the CEOs I've worked with and interviewed. When your company is growing and has been growing for years, it's hard to expect or believe anything other than continued growth. However, executives need to be aware of the possibility of a decline and make sure they have in place and are paying attention to the KPIs that provide them an early warning signal that trouble is ahead.

---

[13] I've done my best to remedy this sad fact by writing a book called *Private Equity Investing in Direct Selling: Identifying Risks & Rewards*, which is available here: https://www.amazon.com/Private-Equity-Investing-Direct-Selling/dp/1733356800/ref=sr_1_1?keywords=brett+a.+blake&qid=1572981131&sr=8-1

WHY SALES AND PROFITS AREN'T ENOUGH

You might be asking, "Why do I need KPIs? Won't my sales and/or profits be enough to signal trouble?" Perhaps, but not always. Sometimes sales can be a misleading KPI since many companies continue to have increasing sales (Growth by Promotion) even as the new customer/distributor count is declining (signaling declining sales in the future). For example, I interviewed one CEO of a direct selling company that had been the sweetheart of the channel. In that interview, he told me that his business had been in decline for more than a year before his team acknowledged that they were actually in trouble. This executive (who asked to remain nameless) said that his biggest regret was that he had ignored the signs of decline because sales had continued to climb even though new customer and distributor enrollments had fallen.

"I let the sales numbers fool me into thinking things were fine," he said. "I didn't realize until it was too late that the sales growth had shifted from more customers buying to fewer customers buying more."

For this CEO's company, sales had continued to grow because the company's average order size and the sales per distributor had increased. In other words, they were growing via promotions and more new products to existing customers. They were selling more product, but to fewer people. To make things worse, they were recruiting fewer new distributors and customers and so sales increased despite a shrinking distributor and customer base.

A similar thing can happen with cash. As a company no longer has a need to invest heavily to support exponential growth, the company can see a short-term surge in cash. This is a result of sales declining or growing at a slower pace, but growth-related expenses ending abruptly. Available cash increases for all the wrong reasons even though margins and profits begin to fall. What manager would not be thrilled to have sales growth (even though it is slower growth) and a sudden plethora of cash?

[14] https://www.dispatch.com/news/20170917/retail-watch-thirty-one-gifts-says-its-on-rebound, accessed August 8, 2019.

THREE KPIs YOU CAN'T AFFORD TO IGNORE

If sales and profits are poor ways to assess the future health of a direct selling company, then what KPIs properly signal that a company is heading toward slow growth or no growth? I have interviewed dozens of CEOs and some of the industry's top consultants to come up with what I believe are the big three KPIs that should serve as your advanced warning system.

THE ADVANCED WARNING SYSTEM KPIs ARE:

1. *Net Active Distributors:* The number of distributors who have personally produced volume or recruited new customers/distributors in the last month.[15]
2. *Number of Rank Advancements:* Total distributors who advanced to a new rank.
3. *Net Promoter Score (NPS)*: A simple one question survey, administered on a consistent basis, that gives you directional data on the field's enthusiasm for sharing your products. Administering this by cohort (all distributors who join in a month would be a cohort) can give you even more valuable data over time. The NPS asks customers and distributors to answer the following question using a ten-point scale (0 = Very Unlikely, 10 = Very Likely):

NET PROMOTER SCORE QUESTION

"Considering your complete experience with our company, how likely would you be to recommend us to a friend or colleague?"

Of these three KPIs, the NPS will be your best long-range tool to signal that a problem is coming. Companies that deploy this tool early can begin to see around a corner and predict slowing sales months before their P&L will reveal a problem. Net Active Distributor

---

[15] I attribute this KPI to Winfield Consulting.

numbers will be your second (or your medium-range) warning system and often rank advancements will lag behind distributor activity but precede declining sales.

ADVICE FOR FIELD LEADERS

A Field Leader's Warning System

Most field leaders will not have the resources to administer a Net Promoter Score, but they can still track the activity of their team. Field leaders should track three KPIs for their team:

- How many are ordering every month?
- How many are sponsoring?
- How many advancements do you have on your team each month?

Sometimes your numbers will fall from one month to the next, but when you see your numbers declining in one or more categories for three consecutive months, you have a problem that needs to be addressed. Note that the problem may be company-wide or it might be an isolated issue with your team. While most teams decline when a company declines, there are almost always a few teams that continue to grow even while the bulk of the others are lagging. In other words, you can take action to make sure your team performs irrespective of the performance of other teams.

CHAPTER 4: THE RENEWAL C.H.I.S.E.L.—

Six Variables Every Renewal Plan Should Include

"Every block of stone has a statue inside it, and it is the task of the sculptor to discover it."

—MICHELANGELO

The great Michelangelo understood that there was a masterpiece inside every block of stone, and he knew how to use his chisel to rid the statue of the excess material surrounding the work of art he wanted to reveal. Likewise, if a company has once known success, the answer to improved business performance likely can be found within the existing organization, but it often requires executives to chip away the excess programs, politics and people to find the company's compelling core and growth engine. The process is more art than science, but after years of experience in multiple operating and consulting assignments, I've found that there are a common set of variables that must be included in your plan. These variables combine to form the word C.H.I.S.E.L.— not the most visually aesthetic acronym, I'll admit, but the right variables to focus on if you're a CEO leading a turnaround.

I'll introduce you to the variables that make up your turnaround C.H.I.S.E.L. below and then we will talk about each in great detail in the chapters that follow. Here are the variables that require your attention if you are to renew your company's growth:

Cash
Hope
Innovation
Simplification
Expansion
Leadership

- *Cash*—While the C.H.I.S.E.L. variables are not meant to be sequential in order of importance, the first two variables are the most important because they serve as the fuel to power everything else you will want to do. Most of us have been taught that the goal for any business is to produce a profit. Amazon and dozens of successful technology companies have showed us that profits are eventually important, but the only thing that matters is the availability of cash. Simply put, cash is the fuel that allows a company to continue to operate, and during a downturn a company that previously had plenty of cash can find itself in a negative cash position in no time at all.
- *Hope*—If cash is a company's fuel, hope is the field's fuel. Without hope distributors stop recruiting, stop selling and start looking for something else to do with their time. Specifically, field sales representatives need to have hope that the company is the vehicle that will allow them to reach their dreams, and that means that it will be around and still in demand years from now. Often, companies that have a decline in sales, no matter how small, have field representatives who begin to weave and tell stories of long-term decline. These "leaders" and those who believe their stories no longer believe or have hope in their future with that company. Field leaders play an enormous role in preserving and renewing hope, and later we will talk about the things they can and should do to make sure they don't starve their teams of hope, or worse, that their words and actions don't drain hope from their team.

- ***Innovation***—Any turnaround book will discuss innovation as a key ingredient of a Renewal plan. However, in direct selling, innovation too often is applied incorrectly and instead of contributing to Renewal, new products actually accelerate the decline. Too few companies understand that innovation is governed by a company's brand and the selling systems created to empower the field to acquire customers, distributors, and profitable leaders. Therefore, innovation can come in the form of brand renewal, system innovation, rewards and compensation innovation, technology innovation, or product innovation. Product innovation without thought to brand constraints or the system of selling the new product leads to confusion and can actually slow growth. Said more succinctly, if your selling system is designed to sell baskets, don't expect your field to be able to find Renewal if you introduce new jewelry without also introducing a new sales system to help them sell it. The good news is that companies can sequence brand renewal, system innovation, and product innovation to provide multiple ways of stimulating and nurturing new growth.
- ***Simplicity***—As companies grow and add more and more employees, the field begins to see more and more programs, products and promotions. At first all of this "new" is exciting. But before long, so many initiatives, no matter how simple each one seems, become constraining and confusing to the field. As you prepare a plan for Renewal, deciding what not to do is sometimes as important as deciding what to do. Identifying what you will stop doing will also help you decide how to preserve cash.
- ***Expansion***—While most non-direct sellers will point to new products as the primary driver of Renewal, for better or for worse the number one driver of Renewal in direct selling would have to be international expansion. While international expansion is easy to understand, there are opportunities and examples of companies expanding within their current country, finding pockets of growth in

new states, new demographics or new languages. Just like new stores increase sales for brick-and-mortar retailers, new demographic and geographic expansion increases sales for direct sellers.

- *Leadership*—One of the interviews I recently had with the CEO of a company that has experienced a 70% decline in sales reminded me of this last critical variable that takes so much emotional energy to implement and too often is ignored. This critical variable of leadership is most often manifest in just being present with both your employees and your field. Sometimes when things aren't going well and we feel like we don't have all the answers, we prefer to manage our business in solitary, to hunker down alone in our office. Email, text and social media give us the illusion of effectively doing our job, but nothing substitutes for in-person communication and live reassurance from the company's founder and CEO. Most of the time, direct selling founders and CEOs were out in front and on the road constantly during their growth years, but they fail to continue that practice or to reimplement that behavior during their effort to renew their company's growth. In times of crisis, leaders lead live.

Let's deep dive into each of the C.H.I.S.E.L. variables and give you both the understanding and tools you need to successfully lead your company to renewed growth.

CHAPTER 5: CASH—
The Oxygen of Your Business

"For better or worse, cash is the oxygen of your business, and you can't last long in any environment without it."

—NEIL BLUMENTHAL, CEO WARBY PARKER

Most of us think that businesses live or die based on whether or not they are profitable. Turn a profit, live to see another day. Fail to turn a profit and you are done. That world view became outdated quickly in my family when my youngest brother asked me to invest in his first venture, "Know Marketing." Turns out that venture never came close to making a profit, but was transformed into Funding Universe, an idea that won $50,000 in a college entrepreneur contest and found angel investors who provided more capital until they merged with another company and changed the business model enough to attract more investor dollars. More than a decade later, the company, Lendio, is finally profitable and still raising money—now in the tens of millions of dollars. The lesson learned from watching Lendio is the same taught for decades by Amazon… you don't need to make a profit, but you'd better not run out of cash.

CASH DISAPPEARS IN A FLASH

When I talk to CEOs who haven't experienced Hyper-Growth or haven't had to respond to changing economics as their company moves from Growth by Promotion to the Shake-Out stage, they don't understand why I would first focus on the need for cash. For most direct selling companies and in almost every stage of their business lifecycle, cash is so plentiful it's hard to imagine a scenario where they would need more.

Perhaps you'll understand the perspective of a large direct selling company I engaged with just as they moved from Growth by Promotion to Shake-Out. During one of my early conversations with the CEO of this company I asked, "How is your cash position?" My question was almost brushed aside, and the CEO probably thought I was ignorant for even asking such a thing. Two weeks later I asked again, this time making it clear that there was no correlation between the topline sales of the company and the forecast the finance team continued to publish as their benchmark to measure progress. I urged the CEO to ask the CFO to prove to him that he should not be worried about cash. A few days later, the shell-shocked CEO called me to confirm that in fact the company's cash position was not good and unless something changed quickly, they would be in a cash crisis.

Sudden changes in topline sales, especially after a period of lower margin promotion-driven sales, is a cash account's worst nightmare. Often companies that have experienced Hyper-Growth have allowed their payroll to balloon, have initiatives of every size and variety happening, and have entered into some major liability such as a leveraged debt deal or a large real estate investment or lease. None of these choices are an issue for a growing company flush with cash, but when sales begin to fall off and cash slows, it is surprising to see how often—and how quickly—the company's cash position turns negative.

Whether you refer to it as fuel or oxygen or use a runway analogy, if a company has any hope of surviving a downturn and renewing growth, it will need time and money to figure things out. In my experience it often takes more than one small tweak to renew growth, so making sure the company has cash on hand and some to spare must become the CEOs first and most urgent task. Too often, companies deny that they are in decline or convince themselves that things will return to growth with just a little fine-tuning or a new product launch coming in a few months, so they delay making major cost cuts. Rarely does their optimism pay off. Instead they are forced to make more significant cost cuts to ensure the company survives.

Recently I received a phone call from an executive of a well-known direct seller who told me she had been promoted just a few months prior and had been encouraged to hire a team to join her. She hired great talent who left promising jobs, but less than six months later the founder asked the executive to fire her team because the company couldn't afford them.

"How could they let me hire those people if things were so bad?" she asked. My response was simple: cash positions change very quickly. Far too often, companies make financial commitments (like hiring new employees), before they have truly assessed their cash position. When the reality of how little cash they now have becomes apparent, they are forced to make abrupt cuts in expenses and employee headcount.

THREE-STEP FORMULA FOR CASH MANAGEMENT

As soon as the company's early warning signals point to a downturn in sales, I recommend engaging in a simple three-step formula I call AIM. Focusing on this formula will help companies do all they can to make sure there is plenty of cash to allow for Renewal. The formula is straightforward:

(1) Accurately forecast your true cash position
(2) Identify all sources of cash available
(3) Make operational changes to free cash

ACCURATELY FORECAST YOUR TRUE CASH POSITION

Most businesses have learned to use budgets and plans to communicate progress against some predetermined expectation. The board believes the company should deliver 10% (or 100%) growth and a budget and plan is put in place showing how that will happen and employees are then given that budget as their benchmark to measure success. Forecasting often accounts for the company's current position but is adjusted against the original budget, usually after consulting sales and marketing to learn how they are going to magically make up for any lost ground.

When I walk into a company in decline, almost without exception I find a sales forecast that is completely detached from the reality of current sales trends. It is shocking to see how often plans are still expected to be executed against the budget that is supported by that false forecast.

Companies with a forecast based on an outdated budget or one inflated by sales optimism, marketing, or even the CEO, are often blind to potential cash dangers. If your company begins to see any early warning signals that slower growth or declining sales are approaching, make sure someone begins to provide you with a forecast stripped of all optimism and 100% based on a trendline that reflects sales since the noted change in your early warning signals. Not only do you need a forecast of topline sales, but you also need to see an accurate cash forecast that includes the topline sales trend and any significant changes in costs that might occur when your company's order levels decline and vendors reprice your products accordingly.

> **VALIDATE YOUR CASH POSITION**
> Ask your CFO or controller to:
> - Provide you a revenue forecast based only on the actual trends since your early warning signals changed,
> - Verify that your COGs are accurate, that the price you will be paying for products when you are ordering fewer units is the same or is adjusted in your financial model, and,
> - Provide you a cash forecast that reflects the information gathered above.

USING COHORT DATA

The most accurate forecasts use cohort data to predict future topline sales. Cohort data forecasts begin by comparing the activity of all distributors who enroll in a specific month to the activity of groups enrolled in previous months. Cohort data measures distributor activity by the number of months they are involved and provides a great way to predict the future. Over time, cohort data gives you average activity in sales, purchases and sponsors from one month to the next. For example, if you have 100 distributors join in May (month 1) and by month 5, historic averages predict that those 100 distributors will produce $5,000 in sales (based on all their combined activity), you can predict that if there are only 50 distributors who join in June, then by month 5 that cohort will only produce $2,500. Adding all cohorts together will give you a forecast for coming months that can predict how today's slower sponsoring numbers will impact sales months from now.

FORECASTING THE BOTTOM OF THE DECLINE

One of the most difficult challenges for companies in decline is to both forecast and find the "bottom" of the decline. There are hundreds of variables that can impact how far a company can decline and the stories and experiences we documented in an earlier chapter from Herbalife and Longaberger show that the decline can be short-lived or can continue all the way through bankruptcy. Many companies have declined and found a steady state from which they grew or maintained their position from year to year. Ideally, a company would be able to make a forecast of their leveling-off point and target their initial cuts to go deeply enough to allow them to be cash flow positive should sales reach that level. Below are a few suggestions to help companies predict the bottom of their decline.

Speculators vs. Builders

Traditionally, companies in Hyper-Growth attract two types of people: (1) loyal business builders who are excited about the products and/or the company's mission, and (2) speculators who join because they don't want to miss out on a chance to win big. A few of the speculators will build a substantial business or will fall in love with the company's product and mission, but many will not. One would assume that these speculators will be among the first to leave the company if growth stalls or sales decline. Theoretically, if you could identify how many of the company's distributors were loyal business builders vs. speculators, you could make a reasonable estimate of how far the company's sales will decline before stabilizing.

While most people won't raise their hand and label themselves a speculator, I have seen quantitative research from companies that have asked distributors their primary reasons for joining. This is useful information to have. One might assume that those who claimed to have joined the company either for love of product or love of mission will probably stick around during a downturn, while those who joined to earn extra income or for the business opportunity might be at a greater risk of leaving. If those assumptions were correct and the survey said the company had 70% loyal business builders and 30% speculators, forecasters might project that they would see sales fall at least 30% when speculators drop out. In other words, solid quantitative research can help forecasters predict how deep any cuts might need to be.

Full-time Income Earners

Another model that forecasters could use to try and determine the bottom of a downturn is to identify those distributors who are and have consistently been earning a full-time income from the company (you can identify whether a rank or a specific income level defines full-time). Once it is determined how many full-time income earners you have, you might assume that they have an extra motivation to maintain their income and their will to maintain could be the company's backstop. This forecasting method follows these steps:

(1) Identify "full-time income earners."

(2) Classify these income earners by their current rank.

(3) Further classify the "full-time income earners" by the rank they most frequently qualified at for the past six months (not their highest earned rank).

(4) Forecast what the company's sales would be if each of these leaders were to qualify at their reclassified rank by using the minimum sales required at each rank, making sure not to double count volume for leaders who are nested within another leader's organization.

Sales produced to qualify these full-time income earners at their reclassified rank, assuming minimum requirements to meet the rank, provides another "worst case scenario" forecasting tool.

Maintaining Rank

The final forecast model is to apply the "solid at rank" or "soft at rank" criteria defined in Step 3 above to all distributors who have earned a rank. Then calculate total volume for the company if all of the company's leaders maintained their reclassified rank.

Use More than One Model

Your forecast of future cash flows is likely to be more accurate if you use more than one model. The goal is to be as accurate as possible to avoid requiring the company to commit to cash acquisitions strategies that negatively impact shareholders or employees and to avoid multiple rounds of reforecasting and subsequent rounds of fundraising or expense cuts. Once management has a realistic cash forecast, they can begin to determine where they will get the cash they need during their Renewal period.

Identify Sources of Cash

Most companies spend a lot of time thinking about cash during the start-up phase, but if they go through a period of Hyper-Growth it is often assumed that they will no longer need to worry about sources of cash. The truth is that many companies need additional cash to fund Hyper-Growth and finding cash during a downturn becomes a critical concern for almost every company. Companies source cash from operations, debt (including vendor terms) and equity investors or current shareholders. Unfortunately, by the time a company needs debt and equity (aside from the Launch phase), it is often too late to get them... especially on favorable terms. We will spend most of our time on how to find cash from operations, but let's talk about debt and equity for those companies that have experienced or will experience growth and have not yet seen a downturn.

DEBT

Direct selling companies have traditionally shunned debt and actually used the "debt free" claim as a selling advantage in recruiting. Clearly it is better to be debt free than to be saddled with debt. However, company executives would be wise to seek access to debt when they don't need it and when cash is plentiful. The best time to apply for a line of credit is when you don't need one. CEOs should direct their CFO or finance team to continually shop for more and more favorable lines of credit in larger and larger amounts.

I've seen CEOs who promote accountants or controls to their most senior finance position in the company because they use them primarily for reporting. However, having a good CFO or access to a former CFO (on your board, for example) can be extremely valuable when the time comes to secure debt, equity or other sources of cash.

Bank Debt

Debt is admittedly difficult for direct selling companies to secure versus their non-direct selling counterparts. Most lenders don't understand the channel well and traditionally have been reluctant to lend to companies operating within it. However, many companies do have helpful lines of credit. Some have found a local bank that has bought into the owner's vision; others have found national lenders.

When looking for sources of bank debt it is important to understand that business lending is very different from personal lending. When you apply for a personal line of credit, a mortgage or an auto loan, the lenders are able to access your personal credit score from one or more credit bureaus. Your credit score is an equalizer that allows all lenders to use a simple formula for deciding whether or not to allow you to borrow and at what rate.

Businesses—especially newer businesses and those that have not borrowed in the past—don't have a credit score that can be used to measure their credit worthiness. Lenders, therefore, have to hire underwriters who become expert at evaluating specific types of business credit products. Large lenders may offer a broad spectrum of business loans while smaller ones may be forced to specialize in a certain type of business loan like commercial real estate, inventory factoring or medical equipment loans. It's important for you to understand each lender's specialties because if you don't you may be turned down... not because your business can't qualify, but because the lender you have approached doesn't have expertise in the type of loan you're seeking or in your industry. Keep applying, and spend time up front asking lenders about their specialties—or use a business loan broker who will have relationships with several lenders and can guide you to those who will lend to businesses like yours.

Many first-time business borrowers are forced to personally guarantee a loan for their business. This is your lender's way of saying, "I don't have the expertise to properly ascertain whether or not this loan meets our standards, but I can use your credit score to figure out how much you can borrow and at what rate." If you are working with a local lender it is a great idea to get a line of credit even if you have to personally guarantee it. Ask the lender to agree that this first line of credit will be the first step in preparing your business to have a loan you do not have to personally guarantee. Once you have the line of credit, borrow when you don't need it, and pay it back several times during the term of the loan. Doing so will give the lender more confidence in your business and will make it easier for that lender to allow you to convert to a line that doesn't require your personal guarantee eventually.

Suppliers as Financing Partners

Don't forget that traditional lenders are not your only source of debt. Some of the industry's best success stories are of companies that found suppliers who believed in their future, valued their business and were willing to provide terms for product and raw ingredient purchases. Often vendors are more easily able to access traditional lending and pass that debt through to their direct selling clients in the form of more favorable terms.

Having suppliers who become financing partners might require you to become loyal to that specific supplier. In other words, you will have to move from a multi-source purchasing strategy to a single source supply strategy. This means that instead of shopping for price, you will need to shop for reliability, dependability, ability to scale and willingness to commit to helping your business if and when Hyper-Growth makes it difficult for you to continue to pay on the most favorable terms. A single source supply strategy requires that you learn to share more information sooner and that you have an agreed-upon way of making sure pricing is always competitive (which is not always the same as the lowest). But as I learned in a discussion with a senior supply executive with one of the world's largest tech manufacturers, single source supply strategies are always the most advantageous to companies that have unpredictable patterns of sales, companies that are not disciplined enough to follow a long product development process, and those that want to have access to a supplier's best R&D and new technologies. If you believe cash will be an issue as you grow (and it most likely will), now is the time to start deepening your partnership with your best and most reliable supplier.

Friends and Family

In a recent meeting with several direct selling CEOs, I learned that many had raised debt with equity-like deals they put together with family and friends. One CEO said she asked several friends for $1,000 loans and agreed to pay a premium from the then-prevailing loan rates.

For that premium she had the right to pay interest only or to retire all or some of the debt whenever she elected to do so. This CEO's company has become very successful. She is able to retire all of this friends-and-family debt if she chooses to, but she has allowed a few of the friends to continue to receive their premium interest rate payments each year as her way of thanking them for taking a chance on her and her business.

Borrow When You Don't Need the Cash

Individuals and business owners have learned that lenders prefer to lend to entities that don't need their money. They aren't in the speculation business and want to loan money only when it is almost certain they will be paid back with interest. Wherever you choose to find debt, remember to secure it before you need it and don't wait until you're certain that you won't survive without it.

EQUITY

Another option for raising cash is to sell ownership or equity in your company. An equity offering is often the only way for companies in the Launch Stage to raise cash to fund operations, but that is not true of companies that have or are going through the Hyper-Growth stage.

Equity can be sold to friends and family, to professional investors or to public shareholders via one of the available stock exchanges. Equity is often sold when future cash flows are too uncertain to guarantee a company's ability to satisfy debt repayment or interest payments, or might be an option if a founder or founders feel that it is in their best interest to have a long-term partner who can bring expertise they need but can't afford to pay for with cash.

Recently I received a phone call from the co-founder of a young and growing direct selling company who was already thinking about how to fund what was starting to look like Hyper-Growth. He had resolved that he should focus on selling equity and concluded that they would eventually want additional expertise to help them so gaining that expertise by finding an investor seemed like the rational choice. I told this founder that in my opinion, selling equity in your company should be a last resort. Few professional investors have expertise in direct selling and those with the expertise he lacked could be easily engaged as a consultant or by organizing an advisor board with a reasonable retainer offered to those who agree to serve.

There are perhaps sound reasons to sell equity, but doing it chiefly to acquire expertise is rarely the right decision.

PRIVATE EQUITY INVESTORS

Once a firm gets beyond start-up capital, they often search for private equity investors to help them professionalize their business. The expertise provided by these firms can be helpful on many levels and Herbalife's early experience after the death of founder Mark Hughes is an example of how the right financial partners can help a company prepare to scale. Private equity firms can also help companies gain access to debt providers and might have additional investment dollars in their funds that can be used to assist a company in later stages. In fact, most of the owners who choose to sell equity to a private equity partner do so with liquidity (short-term and long-term) as a primary objective and it is probably true that private equity partners have expertise when it comes to deciding how to maximize the value of your business.

Unfortunately, too often, private equity investors have either purchased a company with a little equity and a lot of debt or have encouraged founders to leverage the company's future earnings to fund near-term distributions with debt. Companies saddled with debt before they enter the Shake-Out stage have even more cash constraints. This problem in the channel is yet another reason why I wrote the book I referenced earlier, *Private Equity Investing in Direct Selling*, just to try and prevent these tragic transactions. There are far too many examples of companies who were either forced into bankruptcy or liquidation, or forced to lay off way too many employees shortly after a downturn because they didn't have the cash to meet debt obligations and operating needs.

If you choose to sell equity during the boom times, prepare for the bust by making sure you leave some cash reserves in the company and have additional access to capital (debt or equity) on favorable terms. These reserves could be distributed and held by the owners in other accounts (to keep management from being wasteful), but ideally current shareholders will have cash reserves available to respond to a call for cash from the company in times of need.

ACCOUNTS PAYABLE

For many direct selling companies, channel partners can be a critical part of a financing plan. There are several examples of direct sellers leveraging relationships with good vendors to pay for their rapidly expanding inventory needs. Likewise, excellent vendor partnerships can become a valuable resource to companies that experience short-term cash shortages. These partnerships on rare occasions can produce actual cash in the form of debt, but typically the help comes in the form of:
- Holding inventory ordered but not needed,
- Extending the terms and allowing companies more time to pay for inventory delivered,
- Renegotiating real estate or equipment lease terms,

- Reselling or repurposing raw ingredients to allow a company to avoid paying for goods ordered but no longer needed.

Some companies force their suppliers to wait for payments without properly communicating with them. While this might help you meet your cash obligations in the short-term, remember that companies that make it through their period of Renewal often experience significant growth in future years. Having suppliers that are good partners who want to help you meet demand in the future are preferred to suppliers that begrudge your business. Perhaps a true story from the experience of two large technology companies will best illustrate the importance of good partnerships with your vendors. The story is true, told to me by the head of the supply team, but I've concealed the names to protect confidentiality.

Tech Company A and Tech Company B had decided to partner to create a product together, but each company maintained its own supplier base and purchasing department despite the joint venture they formed for this partnership. Several years into the project, the joint venture found itself in desperate need of accelerating a new product and both companies put their purchasing departments to work trying to figure out if they could meet the new timeline. Tech Company A prided themselves in their ability to work one set of suppliers off the other and maintained a fairly aggressive and somewhat adversarial relationship with their vendors. Tech Company A came back to the table and said, "We've completed an exhaustive review of our supply chain and we see no way of delivering this new product in less than eighteen months."

Tech Company B had a much different relationship with their suppliers. Instead of working one off the other, they identified vendors they could trust and invested in making them better. The company actually had an investment fund they used to help suppliers make needed improvements in capital and equipment. Tech Company B reached out to their suppliers and explained the opportunity and engaged them in a dialogue about how to accelerate the timeline. Tech Company A was in disbelief when Tech Company B's purchasing department returned with the news that their supply chain could ramp up and have the product available in three to six months.

Establishing strong relationships and continuous open communications with vendors is both a long-term competitive advantage and the best approach to enroll their help in meeting your short-term cash needs.

Make Operational Changes to Free Cash

All companies, even those with access to debt or equity, will need to pay attention to their cash from operations in the event of downturn in sales. Below we will talk about the many ways of improving a company's cash position and provide some helpful tips along the way.

CUT COST "TOO SOON" AND "TOO FAR" AT FIRST

My advice to CEOs entering the Shake-Out stage is to make rapid and deep cuts to the organization as soon as the Net Promoter Score and Net Active Distributor numbers confirm that you are in or entering decline. Too often, companies make too few cuts in the number of employees and the number of initiatives happening in the company and instead of having one painful experience, the company is subjected to dozens of "D-days" as they go through one round after the next of cost-cutting layoffs. Having experienced that pain, I recommend you allow your current trends to drive your forecast and with no optimism. Determine what your worst-case scenario looks like and then right size your organization to be profitable at that level of sales. Your employees and field leaders will be much more excited to hear about a needed round of rehires than to hear weeks or months later that you need to make yet another round of cuts.

CREATE CASH-BASED INCENTIVES

Most companies have incentive programs that reward management for meeting revenue and/or profit objectives. Unfortunately, these incentives typically do little to preserve or increase a company's cash on-hand. Wise CEOs and boards should make changes to their executive compensation to focus incentives on cash rather than profits. Paying a modest bonus to executives, even when the company is declining and not producing a profit, is a smart investment if it results in significantly improving the company's cash position.

BENCHMARK COSTS

Once you have a true and accurate forecast of your topline, you can use that number to help you establish what your costs must be in order to have a positive cash flow. It can be helpful to benchmark your costs by comparing your current costs, organizational structure, number of employees, and programs to those you had in place when you hit that number the first time. In other words, if you grew to $200 million in sales and expect that you are on your way to a decline that will end around $150 million, then compare your current cost structure to the costs you had when you reached $150 million in sales the first time. You will probably be shocked at how many additional people and programs you have added, and you'll also be encouraged by the profitability the company had previously at $150 million.

"MUST FUND" TACTICS AND STRATEGIES

Remember that Renewal is not simply a practice of reducing expenses. It requires companies to execute strategies and tactics that will lead to growth again. If you are confident in those strategies and tactics then make sure you preserve the people and cash required to succeed. If you don't know exactly what will be required, expect that you will have a demand for investment dollars. Make sure your cuts will free cash and your reduction in your workforce will leave bright people to help you find the programs and products required for growth.

"NICE TO HAVE"

Good people, good programs and "nice to have" resources are the enemies of success. Cutting expenses will be painful and executives need to have a survivor's mentality when reviewing the many, many good options that they will want to keep. If you believe in a program that has been introduced and you're still in decline, chances are you don't need it. If you are working on a program that you expect to provide only incremental improvement, chances are you can't afford it. Sometimes it helps to remind yourself that companies that experience Renewal will have the opportunity to return to a cash position that will allow some of these projects to return. In the short-term, follow the mantra *When in doubt, do without.*

INVOLVE YOUR TEAM

Senior executives tend to worry that there are members of their team who are not capable of making the tough decisions needed to return the company to a position of positive cash flow. Some might even suspect that the executives should be fired as part of the inevitable round of layoffs. I believe that it is critical to get input from every corner of the company and to be open to ideas and opinions that you may not have considered. Because of my bias for broad input, I believe it is critical to give every member of your team the assignment to produce a plan that will reduce expenses. Often their ability to think strategically and to make necessary cuts to their team will surprise you. However, a team member's failure to make a meaningful contribution to this process is also useful information to have and can make it easier for you to decide to move forward without them in the future.

It is almost impossible to succeed in renewing a company when painful cuts to people and programs have been mandated by a single executive or a few executives at the top. The best outcomes involve a team working together to find solutions they can agree on, and to make sacrifices they understand and are personally committed to make.

PRICING AND MARGIN ENHANCEMENT

Almost without exception, companies in decline have financial executives who begin to look at ways of improving cash and margins by increasing the price of their products or by reducing incentives in some way. In other words, the company wants its customers and sales representatives to pay for the over-hiring and indulgences of company management and staff. Sometimes price increases are warranted, but just as often an increase in the price of products or the elimination or reduction in distributor incentives makes things worse, not better. If you decide to consider a price increase, make sure you employ the discipline of benchmarking your pricing with that of similar products available in other channels. If your retail price is not competitive, logic would argue that consumers will vote with their checkbook to the further detriment of your company.

My caution is not to be interpreted as an absolute rejection of pricing and commissions changes. When I was a young executive at USANA Health Sciences, we successfully turned sales around on the back of a price value initiative that both increased margins, decreased prices and reduced commissions on a per-product basis. Notice that we improved margin as we DECREASED price. Our rationale for decreasing per-product commissions was based on the belief that lower prices would make our products easier to sell and that customers would likely purchase more. That theory turned out to be correct.

Another important part of the strategy we followed at USANA was focusing our R&D on reformulations that combined some products and reduced SKUs in a way that added more value and improved margin. These tactics were very successful and helped the company not only delight our public shareholders, but also give our field more confidence in their ability to share our products with customers. They helped us increase sales and sponsoring after two years of declining or flat sales. Margin improvements via more intelligent pricing and distributor incentives is possible, but the focus should be on consumer value, not on a just increasing price or reducing incentives for the sole sake of improving margin.

REVISIT YOUR COST OF GOODS

As we've discussed, it is typical for direct sellers to transition from the Hyper-Growth stage to the Growth by Promotion stage marked by the introduction of discounting and promotions to continue growth when sponsoring slows. Because of this discounting, by the time the company begins to respond to decreasing cash flows in the Shake-Out stage, the natural tendency is to find a way to respond to the lower margins they have been experiencing. Wisely, companies begin to look for ways to decrease the amount of product sold on promotion. In addition to promotion disciplines, companies should begin to look carefully at their costs of goods. Two things tend to happen as a company's growth begins to slow:

(1) Companies are able to take the time to re-evaluate their supplier contracts. Often, they have failed to renegotiate their supplier contracts despite a significant increase in volume from when they were initially put in place.
(2) Companies that have pricing based on higher order volumes will find that they are ordering less product less often. These companies may be using cost of goods numbers based on the higher volume discounts, but in fact they are being charged much higher prices because their order volumes have not met negotiated minimums.

Making sure your financial model is capturing the accurate cost of goods is essential and having your team work with vendors to figure out how to maximize margins at the new lower volume order levels is critical. A small improvement in the per unit cost of items sold can make a significant improvement in cash flow and is much easier than many other operational ways of improving your company's cash position.

PLUG THE CASH CONSUMING HOLES

Too often executives struggle to find ways to free cash by eliminating employees they don't want to lose when they could save much more if they would simply plug cash consuming holes in their operations. For example, here are two holes that needlessly consume cash:

1. **Credit Card Processing Fees:** Often companies believe they have negotiated credit card processing fees less than 3% when in reality their processor is adding dozens of additional fees that result in the company paying 1% to 1.5% more. Auditing your credit card processing fees can be difficult, but it's a simple exercise for trained professionals. I have arranged for a consulting group to perform a FREE CREDIT CARD PROCESSING AUDIT for the readers of this book. If you would like to see how much your company is paying, take a minute now to fill out the online form found at the URL below, and I'll have an expert provide you a FREE, NO OBLIGATION CREDIT CARD PROCESSING AUDIT for your company: https://www.sidefactor.com/ccaudit/

2. **Copier and Printing Fees:** I was shocked to learn that one of the most expensive variable costs companies have is something most don't think about—the expense of copies and prints. Most companies can save enough to keep at least one full-time employee, and some can save enough to keep dozens of employees. Again, auditing your expenses is FREE and easy, and I have arranged for an expert consultant to offer a free audit to all of my readers. If you are interested, complete the simple form online: https://www.sidefactor.com/free-printing-audit/

STOP, OR AT LEAST SLOW, NEW PRODUCTS

Direct selling executives must always remember that most new products are cash consumers. Too many products introduced too quickly will make it more costly to grow (you have more to buy to keep up) and consumes cash on the way down. Too many direct selling companies have taken cash from their bank accounts, converted that cash into inventory and now store it in their warehouse. Eventually some (hopefully most) of that inventory will be turned back into cash at a great return, but too often new products do not lead to new sales and companies learn they could have had the same revenue with fewer SKUs. If you don't find discipline during your growth, find it during your decline and be extremely deliberate so that you avoid spending your valuable cash on inventory that doesn't drive a short-term return. Here are a few tactics other leaders have employed:

1. Instead of adding new products in large quantities, introduce fewer products at a time and allow distributors to focus on a few.
2. Spread out your product launches. One top company executive moved from two catalogs a year to four and spaced out her new products to reduce the requirement for large cash outlays twice a year.
3. Reformulate and introduce "new and improved" versions of existing products. Adding news the field can talk about without increasing the number of SKUs in your warehouse is a cash plus.

REDUCING HEADCOUNT

Cutting employee costs is often required to bring a direct selling company back into a positive cash position. Again, benchmarking headcount to the period of time when you first met the forecasted revenue amount is a great place to start. Often companies begin to increase their legal and HR departments as they grow and enter more of a "protectionist" mentality for their business. So too, the marketing, sales, and customer service departments expand during the Hyper-Growth stage to allow the company to take on more projects and deliver more programs. Said another way, when you have more employees, you also have more projects and programs being created by those employees to justify their existence. These additional programs increase costs and one of the best ways to eliminate those costs is to reduce headcount so that there are not enough people to continue all of the programs. Be clear with the remaining employees that you do not want them to continue to do all you have been doing. Make sure that you specifically empower the remaining employees to go through an exercise of answering the question, "What can we no longer do well with the number of employees we currently have?" Ask to see the resulting list and encourage your teams to reduce and simplify.

For better or for worse, I have been forced to lay off more employees than most executives, and have thereby earned the right to offer you a little advice about the process...

Rehire Your "A-Players" before You Lay Off Others

Before you inform the entire company that you are going to have layoffs, or even right before you begin layoffs, take time to rehire your "A-Players." Remember that your best employees are also the most employable—meaning other companies would gladly hire them should they become available. In fact, too often, great employees end up leaving a company after a round of layoffs just because they didn't know the company thought they were great and they assumed they would be let go soon as well. While you can't (or at least shouldn't) tell someone you won't ever lay them off, you can sit down with the best talent you have and let them know that they are great. I would say something like this:

"Jill, as you know, our sales have dropped and we want to make sure the company is healthy while we execute our plan to renew our growth. That means we will have to have layoffs and we are planning to announce those layoffs later today. I wanted to meet with you first, and make sure you know that you are NOT on our list. In fact, you are one of our most valued employees and I am counting on your help during this period of renewal. I believe we will figure this out and will grow again. We see you as a critical part of our future."

Then you should ask them: "Will you be willing to stay through this Renewal and be part of my team?"

It is possible that some will open up and express their plan or desire to leave. It's best for you to know that as soon as possible. If they are going to leave and make it clear that you can't save them, you then have the option of including them in the current round of layoffs.

Respecting Those Who Leave

Remember, if your Renewal plan is successful you will be hiring again, and how you treat people on their way out will impact the company's ability to hire great people again in the future. I recently spoke with an executive of a top tech company who told me that their CEO was forced to fire two attorneys with seven figure salaries only to rehire those same attorneys six months later. You never know when you will need the people you don't need today. I believe respecting those who leave includes:

1. *Informing Them in Person*—don't have a mass layoff with letters distributed in bulk or a room full of people who are leaving. Even if you are firing dozens or hundreds of employees, each one deserves to hear from a supervisor or manager and to be thanked for the contribution they have made.

2. *Proactive Outsourcing*—Wherever possible, reach out to departing employees to see if you (or your team) can recommend them to other potential employers. Early in my career we sold a company and had to make the announcement two weeks before Christmas. We eased the pain of that announcement by inviting several

companies to come to our small office for a "career day" the day after the announcement. I believe that everyone except for me and the CFO had job offers and new jobs before Christmas and enjoyed a silver lining despite the bad news that their current job was going away.

If you can't help place employees who are leaving, you can offer (and suggest to other supervisors and managers) to write a letter of recommendation that clearly outlines to future employers that the employee was not fired for cause but was instead part of a company-wide layoff. This letter will help them more quickly get past any hesitation future hiring managers might have as they learn they were let go by your company.

3. *Don't Make It Personal*—Managers often forget that layoffs are not a result of something the employee did or did not do but are instead a required response to business realities. Unlike the practice of firing an employee for cause, these layoffs need not be adversarial and are not the time to bring up weaknesses that were not enough to lead to termination. Blame the company, not the person... and do all you can in your exit interview or layoff discussion to build the exiting employee's self-esteem.

Communicate to Those Who Stay

If you have followed the recommendations above you will have met with your star employees, but on the day of the layoff it is important for *all* employees to hear from the company. These could be department level meetings or a company-wide meeting, but either way the employees need to hear what has happened so they are not left to speculate. While this communication should be positive and give remaining employees evidence to have hope in the future of the company, I strongly recommend that you do not allow any executive to promise that there will be no more layoffs. It has been my experience that you cannot be certain in making those promises, and if future layoffs are required the management team will have earned very little trust to keep needed employees from leaving.

Cash management is critical at every stage of a Renewal and is not a "one and done" exercise. Even after successfully executing all of the A.I.M. recommendations above, the company's CFO has to monitor cash on a regular basis and be proactive in communicating any anticipated change in the cash forecast immediately so a plan can be put in place to respond to the change.

With cash on your radar screen and a plan to preserve it in place, you are now ready to focus your efforts on fueling your field with Hope.

ADVICE FOR FIELD LEADERS
Supporting Management's Tough Cash Decisions

Most of the time field leaders will not have a direct role to play in helping a company create or execute a plan to preserve cash, but smart field leaders can recognize and support efforts management will make to be wise with the company's cash. When a direct selling company starts to make changes to preserve cash, the field most often is impacted in a way that is negative to them. For example, when you are expecting a catalog with ten new products and it comes out only having eight, it is easy to be disappointed. The field can get even more alarmed when the company that has been hiring for months or years suddenly begins to reduce its employee count. Almost without exception your team will begin to ask if they company "is going to make it."

Wise field leaders will look on management's efforts to preserve cash as a positive sign and will make sure that their team recognizes cuts as indications of good management. More troubling would be a company that ignores signs of decline with no visible efforts to cut back. Help your team understand the lifecycle of a direct selling company and show them how common it is for companies to have a correction after a cycle of growth. Your proactive communication during the Shake-Out stage can shorten its length and help get your company to Renewal more quickly. In my experience, the most significant challenge companies face during a period of decline is rarely the actual business challenges like cash, but the challenge of convincing the field to go back to work. Once the company has taken the action to assure its cash position, the next and most important task is to help field leaders gain confidence and hope for their future.

CHAPTER 6: HOPE—
Fuel for the Field

> "Optimism is the faith that leads to achievement. Nothing can be done without hope and confidence."
>
> —**HELEN KELLER**

Often, one of the first signs of trouble is when a company has fewer new distributors being sponsored. Companies scramble to treat slow sponsoring as if it were a disease that can be cured with a better program, promotion or incentive. In many cases a slowdown in sponsoring is not the disease, but rather a symptom of a more serious ailment—a loss of hope. As soon as a distributor becomes convinced that the company is not the right vehicle to help them reach their goals, they stop having the ability to sponsor others with integrity. In other words, people don't stop sponsoring because they don't know how or don't see the benefit, but rather because they lack the confidence they once had in the business. They lack the conviction that made it easy to invite others to do what they were doing. If they don't believe the company will help them reach their long-term goals, it's incredibly difficult to convince others to join in.

Hope, or the belief that the company or its products will produce the desired result, is the life spring of direct selling. It is admittedly one of those "touchy, feely" things that no one talks about at business school and most avoid talking about with other executives, but it is so foundational to the success of direct selling that it requires not only consideration and conversation but analysis. It can and must be quantified, measured and resourced.

Hope is under constant attack by naysayers of the channel, and if your company and field leaders allow it, rumors and the thousands of lies that are carried on her wings will consume hope and leave nothing but fatigue and bitterness behind. Even in times of growth—but more deliberately in times of decline—your company needs to manage hope with as much attentiveness as you give to your cash accounts.

Founders start their companies with nothing more than a story that inspires hope and belief in their vision of what is possible, and that hope and belief is enough to enroll early employees, investors and distributors. It's not difficult for founders to get out of practice and stop telling their hope-inspiring stories as the demands of Hyper-Growth consume them. Once a company starts to experience headwinds and slowing growth, founders must reassume their role as "Chief Hope Officer." They perform that duty by returning to their early days, dusting off the story of the future and broadly sharing their vision again with employees, shareholders and distributors. Founders must be active and engaged in restoring hope and must fight for resources to protect the company from the enemies of hope.

MEASURING HOPE

More often than not, the Net Promoter Score (NPS) will be the best tool you have to measure the state of hope in your company. If customers believe in your products, they will want to tell others and when distributors have hope that your company will meet their goals for the future, they will want to share the opportunity with others. While the NPS can be a very effective tool to measure hope, it is only useful when measured over time. Companies that begin measuring NPS early can see and respond to changes in that baseline score, while those that only begin using NPS when they suspect there is a problem are left to guess at the early results that come with no benchmark to define good and bad.

If your company is experiencing decline and has yet to deploy NPS to measure hope, there is a way to begin right now: start by identifying those who are currently sponsoring at or near the peak enrollment rate and split off their NPS response as a benchmark against which you measure the rest of the field. In other words, compare the NPS of all of your field to the average NPS of those who are still successfully sponsoring and work to make the two match.

THE H.O.P.E. FORMULA

For most start-ups, little thought is given to creating hope because it is a natural by-product of "selling" others on the founder's vision. Founders are constantly providing stakeholders evidence that their vision is possible. They are sharing stories of product success, business success and even the success of competitors. The natural outgrowth of the company's formulating activities and an output of the success of those activities is an employee base and field sales force that has hope.

As a company matures and experiences successes and failures, founders become operators and often there is no one left to continue to remind stakeholders of the reasons they should continue to be involved. By the time a company recognizes that their field (and employees) are losing hope in their future, the company typically needs a more deliberate formula to restore hope. That formula includes:

- Humbly Listening to Field Leaders—having the humility to listen and be empathetic to legitimate concerns employees and distributors might have.
- Open Communication—being present more often, sharing your awareness of the issues and your plans to improve them AND continuing to tell success stories. Reviving the story of why the company exists and explaining what it has achieved so far and what it can accomplish in the future.
- Plan of Action—the company needs not only a business plan that can inspire hope in the future, but it also needs a plan to address any negativity that starts to consume social media conversations.

- Education—both company and field leaders need to understand that retractions are the norm. There must be a concerted effort to show all the stakeholders how other companies have faced similar slowing and found Renewal and significant growth on the other side.

Let's explore the H.O.P.E. formula in more detail and help you understand how to implement it in your company or team.

Humbly Listen to Field Leaders (and your team)

History has shown that Hyper-Growth often breeds hubris. Founders, CEOs, top sales leaders and even corporate executives and staff often equate their success to all things positive. They begin to believe that their company has found the secret keys to success; that other companies don't have their wisdom, talent, skills, and people. Sometimes this conceit prevents the organization from perceiving the common issues that start and then accelerate a company's decline.

Earlier in my career I joined a company that had seen significant success and created dozens of financially secure field leaders. The company was justly proud of what they had accomplished and the reputation they had gained along the way. However, by the time I came onboard, sales had dropped by nearly 40% in just two years, and there was no sign of rock bottom any time soon. What surprised me most about this company was the confidence the management team had in the tactics they had unsuccessfully deployed over the previous few years.

Fortunately, I had not experienced the wild success of the past, but instead was asked to lead the Renewal of today. I started where I believe every leader should start: by traveling to host listening sessions with sales leaders. They had experienced the success of the past but were also on the frontline of selling and sponsoring today. The sessions I had with dozens of leaders in each town shocked them. I had not come to teach, not come to motivate, and not come to tell. I had come to listen.

As the CEO, I always wanted to be the one to conduct field listening sessions. In nearly every case where I've deployed this tactic, I've found the answers... or at least identified the key issues we had to address to reach Renewal. However, it might be impossible for a founder or CEO to make him/herself this vulnerable to criticism. If that is the case, I suggest you empower someone to listen who can do so without getting defensive. I would send a key executive, board member, or trusted consultant – someone the field will see as having authority to impact change and someone with patience and wisdom.

If you will be humble enough to start by listening, your path to Renewal will be shorter and you will know you are addressing the right issues. You will also be preparing the ground for a renewal of hope because field leaders will leave those sessions convinced that you care and that you have heard them. When they know you have heard them, they will begin to believe that you will make things right again. Hope is renewed when leaders and teams are humble enough to listen empathetically and with real intent to those they lead.

Open Communication

Open communication with the field requires corporate leaders to walk the tightwire and find a balance between transparency and inspiration. At times I have been too transparent and left field leaders completely without hope. Conversely, without transparency it is tough to convince field leaders that you understand that there are problems and that you are committed to fixing them. Great communication strikes the perfect balance and leaves the field certain you understand, and confident you will fix whatever's wrong... eventually.

Sometimes challenges are compounded by the fact that there is not an effective method of communicating with the field. Excellent communication in a direct selling company requires an actual system in place to accomplish it effectively. The sales team needs to know when and how they will receive information. Companies and field leaders typically have more than one system, but they often include weekly calls (always on the same day and at the same time), zoom meetings, monthly newsletters, weekly emails and sometimes a few texts when a message is urgent. If your company has not established predictable communications systems during your Hyper-Growth or Growth by Promotion stage, you MUST do so during the Shake-Out stage.

I learned the value of open communication with field leaders when I took over as the interim General Manager for USANA in Australia and New Zealand. When I arrived on the scene the business was in trouble in almost every imaginable way. Like many executives I've worked with, I arrived in Australia thinking that the field wouldn't know much about the state of the business. Fortunately, I set those thoughts aside and decided to begin weekly calls with all leaders who qualified at a rank equal to full-time income. During my first call I learned two things that have been universally true no matter the country, company or circumstance I've found myself in: (1) the field leaders knew exactly what was happening, way more than they should, and (2) they were grateful for my willingness to speak of the issues with openness and candor.

Each week, I invited my direct reports and these field leaders to join me on a conference call. I would begin each call with a "state of the company" and then I would open the call for questions. The field leader's questions and our ensuing dialogue helped me and my team understand what was most important to field leaders and therefore helped us prioritize tasks and improvements. These calls also gave my team a chance to hear how committed I was to making things right for the field, and that knowledge helped my team align their priorities as well.

It took us weeks to begin to make progress on the field's important issues and even longer to work through very difficult product supply and public relations issues, but that business began to grow for the first time in months within days after that first call. I've seen similar results on multiple occasions in different companies. For many field leaders, the simple action of humbly listening and engaging in consistent and predictable communication is enough to restore their hope and to help them return to work with integrity.

The great truth about hope is that it doesn't require perfect plans, products or execution. It is not even a state of being but rather simply an idea planted firmly in the mind of what is likely to be. The immaterial nature of hope is both good and bad. It always favors the most credible and is often the last voice that deposits information into a willing mind.

Hope always favors the most credible and is often the last voice that deposits information into a willing mind.

Plan of Action

Transparent and honest communication informed by listening with empathy and humility can make an immediate impact on hope and can even lead to hope-inspired activities that can be measured as increased sponsoring and sales. However, eventually that communication runs out of steam if there is not a sound plan and appropriate action to sustain the good feelings. After listening and understanding the critical issues faced by the field and employees, the company needs not only a business plan that can inspire hope in the future, but it actually needs a plan to address the negativity that often starts to consume more and more social media conversations during the Shake-Out stage.

Developing a plan to fix the issues that are holding the company back is critical and communicating that plan to the appropriate people at the appropriate time is a wise business decision. But don't forget to manage expectations and to be clear about what you *know* will work and what you *think* will work. Too often company leaders secure their follower's hopes on a plan that for some reason does not work. The failure of that plan not only delays the company's return to growth, but even more tragically it destroys confidence in management and makes it less likely that the next plan will restore hope or gain the support it needs to succeed.

Here are a few tactics to help you develop and execute a plan to restore hope to your company:

- *Test and Validate*
- *Have a Plan to Fight for Hope on Social Media*
- *New vs. News*

Test and Validate

When communicating your plans, make sure you leave room for testing and validation and set the expectation that changes might be required as you test the plan in the marketplace. I prefer to set expectations by assuring employees and field leaders that "we are going to figure this out together" rather than trying to sell them on the certainty of the first plan we present. Great leaders will share their plan and their intention to validate and refine it, thereby setting the expectation that there will be a time of experimentation. In my experience, the field and employees want to know that you are committed to a fix, not necessarily the one and only fix you and/or your team came up with first.

Have a Plan to Fight for Hope on Social Media

In today's world, it is almost impossible to turn around sales if you don't first turn the tide on social media. Everyone is a social media reporter and unfortunately, they are able to share ideas and opinions whether or not the information has any basis in fact. Direct selling has always had its naysayers but today those who don't like the channel, those who have failed, and those who dislike another field leader, the founders or anything else have a simple way to tell the world. While most of us can easily spot those with an ax to grind, it is very difficult for people to tell what is true, what is half true and what is completely false. You owe it to your field to make sure that the information published on social media is true and that false information is refuted immediately. Even better, you should have a proactive plan to make sure there is a constant flow of good news on social media. Paying for help in producing stories and fighting the naysayers on social media is worthwhile and deserves to be part of a budget, even when times are tough.

I strongly recommend and endorse investing some of your valuable cash in hiring experts to help you ensure that you win the social media battle. Make sure your company looks great on the first page of search results with nothing there to make a prospect fear being involved. Make sure you are monitoring and responding appropriately to social media critics and that you have a plan for overwhelming your social channels with good news. Teach your leaders how and where to vent and don't allow them to use social media—ever—as their place to provide well-intended or ill-intended feedback. It may seem like a waste of money, but if you don't win online it will be tough to generate a positive return on any other investment you would prefer to make.

New vs. News

When I began my career in direct selling, the prevailing wisdom of the industry dictated that a company introduce a new product to excite their field three to four times a year. It didn't take long for companies to figure out that new product introductions were not increasing dollars per distributor/customer, but rather were just increasing costs and tying up valuable capital in inventory. More products also meant more for distributors to learn. Over time, companies began to understand that there had to be a better way.

At USANA Health Sciences, we prepared for the 2002 Winter

Games in Salt Lake City by using our relationship with Olympic athletes to pepper the field with news they could share; news that would make them proud to represent the company and its brand. Along the way, we learned that the field really didn't need new products as much as they just needed something new to talk about. I've become convinced that when companies don't have a plan that feeds good news to the field, the tendency is for the field to fill that communications void with rumors and worries that may or may not be true but will most assuredly destroy hope.

Having a consistent and deliberate plan to create and communicate good news often is a wise move. The more diligent you are at controlling the dialogue, the more difficult it becomes for hope-destroying rumors to find a foothold. Investing in a plan to both combat negative comments on social media and ensure that the field has a constant flow of good news to share with others is a critical and a worthwhile expenditure—even when cash is tight.

Education

Taking time to make sure field leaders understand the stages direct selling companies go through and making sure they have data to support their desire to believe the company will grow again is essential. I'm not a huge advocate of addressing a downward trajectory on the main stage at a convention or as a common theme in communication to the general field, but I do believe straight talk with meaty information is essential for top field leaders. The type of education I'm advocating can often be best presented by a third-party consultant, board member or a non-sales executive like the CFO. This is not information about the company or your plan (though that can often follow), but rather facts and figures from other companies in the channel. Showing four to six company sales charts—using my business phase chart presented early in the book or one like it—and *especially* emphasizing large companies that have had growth and success after a downturn is critical.

This presentation creates fertile soil for other executives to plant the seeds of hope in the form of the company's specific plans for Renewal. If you have a leader's meeting on the calendar, use it. If you don't have anything planned, it is worth the money to bring key leaders together if they have been seeing smaller paychecks month-over-month for more than six months.

ADVICE TO THOSE ON THE CORPORATE TEAM

When things turn from great to good to not-so-good, it is easy to blame others, especially those with a sales title or those who are earning a sales commission. Often corporate staff and employees accelerate the decline in sales by straining the relationship between the company and the field. Renewal happens more quickly when there is respect and plenty of communication and cooperation between the field and the company.

Recently I interviewed Womenkind founder Milan Jensen, who started her career decades earlier at GNLD. She said that during her tenure the company had a strict rule prohibiting any staff member from speaking ill of a distributor.

"We knew that if we were caught saying something negative about one of our distributors, we would lose our job," she said. "This strict rule cultivated a genuine and deep culture of reverence for the field which in turn fueled a high level of trust and carried the company through many difficult shifts in their business."

I would suggest that every direct selling executive, manager and staff member follow that rule even if your company doesn't enforce it. Pointing fingers or assigning blame will only prolong the period of decline and make it more and more difficult to find Renewal. I would encourage every direct selling employee—especially executives and founders—to replace blame with the belief that the field holds the answers to your renewed growth. Do all you can to support them, inspire them... and *listen* to them.

ADVICE FOR FIELD LEADERS

Why Field Leaders are a Key to Hope

The H.O.P.E. formula should be implemented by the founder, CEO or corporate staff, but it can and should also be implemented by field leaders. Field leaders recognize, often before the company's leadership, when their team is starting to lose hope and can begin their own effort to restore it using the same formula I've advocated for corporate leadership. Remember that most of the time there are teams that are able to insulate themselves during a corporate-wide downturn and continue to experience growth in sales, commissions, and advancements. Great field leaders will implement the H.O.P.E. formula and help their team get back on track sooner.

If you are a team leader you are the primary keeper of hope and your role cannot be delegated to downline leaders or the company's executives or founders. Your team's attitude, belief and vision for the future is your responsibility. If you want to meet your long-term goals you must fight for hope at all costs. Great leaders are able to help their team weather difficult periods in the company's history and often will have organizations that are immune to the downturn others are experiencing. Over my many years of observing successful teams in action I've seen great leaders deploy the following tactics to preserve or renew hope:

- *They Have Rules for Team Groups on Social Media*
- *They Are Part of the Solution*
- *They Set and Sustain a Positive Tone*
- *They Don't Try to Become Customer Service*
- *They Take Care of Themselves*

They Have Rules for Team Groups on Social Media

Great leaders don't wait for negativity to emerge. They use social media to communicate and train their team and they also set ground rules for being part of those groups from day one. They teach their team and 1:1 they teach each leader how and where to vent, making it clear that their social media group is not a place to explore negative content. Leaders delete any thread that is designed or has the potential to destroy confidence and hope, and they communicate verbally (by phone or in person) to the offending team member in the spirit of teaching. The first time someone goes negative they earn 1:1 instruction. The second time they are removed from the group.

They Are Part of the Solution

I recently met with a CEO who had seen his large company decline significantly in the past year. We had met early in that decline and I had encouraged him to refocus the company on a simple system of acquiring customers that would be an evolution of the Facebook focus that had brought their initial growth. On this specific occasion the CEO enthusiastically told me of a meeting he'd had with a top leader task force. During that meeting, a leader had asked permission to share with the group some of the success she was having on her team. Given her helpful (versus accusatory) tone, she was allowed to present. The CEO described how this leader had come with a thoughtful presentation that showed what was working, why it was working and how it could scale. She then clearly outlined the changes to current programs and technology that would be required to implement this proven program across the company.

The company is in the process of testing this program as I write this. The CEO expressed to me how grateful he was for a leader who went beyond criticism to actually think through a solution that she had tested with her team. My career has taught me that most (maybe 90%) of the best ideas come from the field, but most field ideas (maybe 90%) aren't scalable or can't be implemented as they are first presented. As a field leader, your company needs your ideas, but even more importantly they need you to test and experiment with your own team so that you can refine and help make the idea work for others.

Don't make your ideas a "do or die" issue for you. Be productive and helpful, but if the company doesn't adopt your concept, be open and teachable to other alternatives. Don't take it personally. The goal is not for you to win an argument but rather to make sure the company finds a way to grow again so that you, your team and everyone else can win.

Set and Sustain a Positive Tone

Great leaders reach out to other crossline leaders and lock arms with them in a commitment to not allow anyone with a negative attitude to highjack their company. Leaders have issues and need someone to talk with, so they create a safe and private place to have those discussions and they always leave with their own hope intact. Just like the water in a river always flows to the lowest point downstream, organizations (of all types) will descend into negativity if allowed to run without proactive leadership. Fighting the natural tendency of your team to turn negative will be a fight that will require significant mental energy. Find confidantes and partners to fight alongside you. Don't try and go it alone, and do hold each other accountable to a high standard of positive leadership. If you lack unity with other crossline leaders, consider working with an outside facilitator who is skilled at working with direct selling leaders. I highly recommend Milan Jensen of Womenkind who has worked miracles with crossline leaders and has decades of personal experience as both a direct selling executive and the leader of a large field team that she and her husband built together.

Milan told me that she learned early in her tenure as a leader how important it was to avoid being drawn into a negative conversation. Milan said, "relationships in the field grow with time, and are often very closely tied to friends and family. When a leader is confronted with someone in their team who is confiding their lack of trust or hope, the leader must listen well and avoid the tendency to feel responsible or obligated to agree, even if you do. Remember, your team member does not really want you to agree. They want to be heard and they want hope from their leader."

Don't Become Customer Service

In every company I've worked with, we have been able to find plenty of positive, capable people to work for an hourly wage (just above minimum wage) to answer the phone and provide customer service. Unfortunately, it is like finding a needle in a haystack to acquire someone who can build, train, and motivate a large team of direct sellers. So, I find it terribly tragic when the few who are capable leaders decide to express their natural urge to serve others by committing to provide personal customer service to their customers or their team. No matter how bad you think your customer service is, you cannot turn in your mantle of leadership for a customer service headset. When the going gets tough, your team needs your leadership. You won't have the time or mental energy to provide that guidance and support if you are the chief customer service officer on your team. Please resist the natural urge to try and fix things that customer service can and should fix.

Selfcare

Take care of yourself so that you have enough emotional energy to take care of others. Only you will know what you need, but whatever your prescription to feel well and to remain happy may be—fill it.

RENEWAL

CHAPTER 7: INNOVATION—
Most Likely Your Key to Renewal

> "Learning and innovation go hand in hand. The arrogance of success is to think that what you did yesterday will be sufficient for tomorrow."
>
> —WILLIAM POLLARD, PHYSICIST & PRIEST

N

My greatest worry in writing this book is that readers will see the word "innovation" and skip the following chapters believing they already understand the content. These readers assume I mean "new products" and may be surprised to hear that I believe new products have as good a chance of leading to further decline than to renewed growth. In the chapters that follow, we will talk about the role of new products and distinguish between the types of new products, but our primary objectives in this chapter are to broaden your innovation palette, to remind you of the limits of your brand and customer acquisition system, and to help you to understand when a new product may also require a new brand and/or a new sales system for distributors to use.

While most executives are focused on new products, most will agree that a company can find Renewal by also considering innovations in:

- The compensation and rewards systems,
- The methods (or system) their field is using to present the product to new customers,
- Renewal of their brand (both its visual look and feel and its promise), and/or
- The introduction of new technology or tech enabled tools.

We will discuss selling systems, product innovation and compensation and rewards innovation in respective chapters to follow, but first let me introduce the concept of innovation boundaries and talk briefly about the opportunities for brand and technology innovation.

BOUNDARIES GOVERNING PRODUCT INNOVATION

In the chart on the following page, I've attempted to provide a simple visual to help you understand that there are boundaries within which we have permission to introduce (and are likely to find success with) new products. Too often, companies that have actually established meaning in their brands in a specific product category—Longaberger in the basket market, for example—will try and redefine their brand as a distribution brand (like Amway, Walmart, Target, etc.) and give itself permission to introduce a wide variety of products. While redefining a brand is possible, especially if you use visual renewal to reset consumer thinking, companies often then run into trouble trying to sell unrelated products because their field has a system for selling Product A and not one for selling Product B.

For example, while Amway established its brand as distributor of multiple brands of products and thereby gave itself permission to introduce almost every product category, their field had not learned how to sell real estate and the system required to sell real estate would have forced the company to introduce an entirely new selling system—not just a new product.

As the visual to the right depicts, the ideal new products will fit between the existing boundaries set by our brand and the selling systems our distributors have been successfully using in the past.

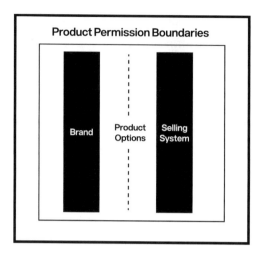

BRAND BOUNDARIES

Most of us understand that brands have meaning. That meaning can grant a company permission to introduce certain products or it may restrict the company from introducing others. For example, Microsoft started as a software operating system but has successfully expanded its brand's meaning so that customers have given the company permission to introduce productivity software (MS Word, PowerPoint, etc.) and eventually computer hardware like the Microsoft Surface. However, if Microsoft tried to introduce a line of football helmets, few athletes would trust the protection of their head to a company with no related experience. While it is possible to extend the expertise of your brand and gain customer permission to produce new products that are related to your core, introducing products that have no clear relationship to your brand only weakens your brand and makes the product a "generic."

BRAND INNOVATION

Brands can and should evolve over time, and it is possible for a company to continue to expand its brand into more and more adjacent categories or to redesign it and attempt to use it to describe an entirely new category. However, there is a caveat, according to Jack Trout of

Brand Strategy Insider.

"When you study the marketing wars," Trout writes, "the well-differentiated specialist tends to be the winner."

Trout believes that specialist brands tend to win for three primary reasons:

1. FOCUS—the specialist brand "can focus on one product, one benefit, one message."
2. EXPERT—the specialist brand is "perceived as the expert or the best. If that's all they do, they must do it very well."
3. CATEGORY GENERIC—"The specialist can become the generic for the category" (e.g. XEROX, FedEx, Google).[16]

In other words, while your brand can evolve over time, it is best if the brand stands as a specialist in something and the evolution is less about expanding its areas of specialty and more about evolving its look and feel to remain visually appealing to today's consumer.

I recommend that companies innovate around their brand in the following ways:

- **VISUAL REFRESH**—If you haven't updated the look and feel of your brand, coupling other Renewal activities with a brand refresh can be an excellent choice. I would avoid the visual refresh prior to other meaningful changes. There is something symbolic about refreshing the look and feel of your brand in conjunction with other Renewal changes that actually are experienced by the field.
- **NEW BRANDS**—If your company is forced to come back from brand-damaging experiences (legal and/or regulatory issues, for example), it may make sense to repackage your Renewal efforts under a new name and brand. However, don't try to rebrand prior to making the meaningful changes necessary to be sustainable.

[16] https://www.brandingstrategyinsider.com/2009/07/the-power-of-the-specialist-brand.html#.XbcwS5NKgW9 accessed 28 October 2019.

Avoid the proverbial mistake of trying to "put lipstick on a pig" and rebrand when you truly are a new and improved version of your company.

TECHNOLOGY INNOVATION

There are a few direct selling companies that define themselves from day one as "technology companies." They have committed to a path that will require them to continue to make technology innovation a central part of their strategy going forward. For the vast majority of direct sellers, technology innovation typically follows system and product innovation but it doesn't lead. I believe technology is important, but rarely should direct selling companies rely on technology innovation to renew their growth. I often hear of companies that want to invest significant dollars in technology before they really understand the customer acquisition system. In my opinion, those companies lock themselves into "systems" that utilize the technology effectively, but don't necessarily drive new growth and sales. Therefore, my advice to most companies is to save their money and avoid developing or acquiring new technology tools until they are clear about the systems they will rely on to grow. Once they know their systems, deciding on what technology they need will be simple and the tools developed or acquired will likely be used.

Let's evolve our innovation options by exploring the role of selling systems, both as a boundary for product innovation and a powerful way to renew growth.

RENEWAL

CHAPTER 8: SYSTEM INNOVATION—
The Most Overlooked Renewal Tool

"You have a great system when everyone knows it, everyone does it, and it works."

—ERIC WORRE, AUTHOR

When I talk about "systems" I'm talking about a recorded way of accomplishing something that eliminates the need for someone to figure out how to do "it" themselves. Author and educator Eric Worre said that you know you have a great system when "everyone knows it, everyone does it, and it works."

I discovered systems accidentally as we grew Team Beachbody from $35 million to $380 million in just three years. Eric Worre, however, helped me by articulating with clarity six specific systems to which I have added one more to make it a lucky seven. In my opinion, the key to exponential growth is for a company (or its sales leaders) to have a few of these seven systems in place:

Direct Selling's Seven Systems:

- **Customer Acquisition**—a simple and repeatable way to start a discussion with a prospect and to convince them to make their first purchase.
- **Distributor Upgrade/Acquisition**—a simple and repeatable way to approach your most enthusiastic customers and convert them to becoming a seller.
- **New Distributor Training System**—a simple and repeatable

way to help a new seller achieve success and confidence.
- **Distributor Advancement System**—a simple and repeatable way of helping new distributors advance to a place of profitability within the compensation system.
- **Convention Attendance System**—this is all Eric Worre and not something I had discovered on my own, but after listening to him I'm convinced that companies need a system in place to get serious distributors to their annual convention.
- **Communications System**—a simple and repeatable way to provide ongoing information and training to distributors.
- **Leadership Development & Training**—a simple and repeatable way to help field leaders acquire the business and management skills necessary to lead a large organization and effectively influence their team.

While I've come to believe there is great value in understanding and methodically implementing all of these systems, it is my experience that growth and Renewal can take place by effectively focusing on the first one: customer acquisition. Therefore, as we talk about innovation, I will particularly focus on the opportunity to innovate and renew the customer acquisition system and even more importantly the critical requirement that new product innovation be restricted to the company's customer acquisition system. Let me explain.

IF YOU'VE GROWN, YOU HAVE A CUSTOMER ACQUISITION SYSTEM

In a phone call with the CEO of a struggling direct selling company, I asked her what the company's customer acquisition system was during peak growth.

"That's the problem," she said. "We don't have a system and never have had a system!"

I knew this company had experienced significant growth and I now know that growth doesn't happen without a system, but the above conversation wasn't the time or place to convince this CEO of that fact. However, I do hope to convince you today.

Every successful direct selling company has a customer acquisition system, but like my CEO friend, surprisingly few executives understand what their system is. That is a bold claim, but years of experience have confirmed it in company after company. How can a company have success and not understand the system that is generating their sales? Often the system driving sales is discovered by the independent sales field leaders. Their experience of trial and error and try again, along with their everyday connection with customers, provides them the perfect opportunity to create, refine and perfect a system of sales. Shockingly few companies have taken the time to learn exactly what their field leaders are using to generate sales. For many (perhaps most) the independent field leaders define the system and teach their teams with little or no support from the company.

One company that didn't initially understand the customer acquisition system developed in the field is Herbalife at the beginning of one of their multiple waves of success. One of the company's waves of success in the United States came as a result of a program developed in Mexico. Rather than attempting to sell a monthly supply of their leading product, Formula 1®, Herbalife's distributors in Mexico offered single servings from their home or workplace and called them "Nutrition Clubs." At first, Herbalife's executives reportedly didn't understand the program and even tried to prevent it from being taught in the U.S. despite the fact that it worked in the Latino communities. Fortunately for Herbalife, they were not successful in stopping this practice and eventually were forced to accept it. Herbalife's impressive growth in the U.S. Latino community started as a result of this distributor-led customer acquisition system that was imported from Mexico by field leaders, and then eventually embraced and supported by the corporate team at Herbalife.

In the spring of 2017, Nu Skin had a sudden and unexpected

revival of sales in the United States. Despite the company's impressive investment in research and development and significant corporate efforts to increase sales, the new sales surge came from an almost forgotten product Nu Skin had been selling for more than ten years. Why? Led by the success of a new distributor in the United Kingdom and follow-on success by a new distributor in the U.S., Nu Skin's field leaders learned how to use social media to share before and after pictures of their decade-old AP 24® Whitening Fluoride Toothpaste to drive demand and increase sales.

Nu Skin executives were wise enough to set aside other initiatives and align behind the momentum of both the product and the social sharing method of selling. Newly appointed Nu Skin CEO Ritch Wood had a sexy, tech-focused strategy to talk about as he took over and the company has followed its field to deploy tech tools designed to support the simple system. As is so often the case, Nu Skin's selling system was accidentally discovered by distributors with a combined tenure of fewer than six months with the company. To the credit of Nu Skin's management team, they were astute enough to recognize and capitalize on the system and reap its benefits.

FAILING TO UNDERSTAND THE SALES SYSTEM CAN LEAD TO SALES DECLINE

Great selling systems are central to the success of direct selling companies, and yet few corporate executives know what system their field is using. Company after company has seen their growth slow and spiral down because executives have made changes to their pricing, product offerings or messaging that inadvertently disrupted the selling system the field was using with success. Even Beachbody saw its growth slow when the company's new digital platform was first introduced without proper consideration given to its impact on the economics and recurring revenue of Team Beachbody Coaches.

Another example of a disconnect between corporate and the field selling system is the rise and fall of skin care direct seller Arbonne.

Arbonne had experienced hockey stick growth as a result of its field's selling system. Field leaders taught their teams to drop off a full skin care system to prospects with this offer:

"I want you to try this amazing product line, and I'm so confident you're going to love this that I'm going to allow you to try it for a week. If you love it, which I think you will, I'm going to stop by next week to pick up a check. If you don't like it, I'll pick up the product and you owe me nothing."

Arbonne's selling system worked and gave new customers and new distributors immediate confidence in the quality of the product. The company grew to more than $800 million in annual sales, but reportedly, their private equity investors followed counsel they received from a consultant with little field experience and a conservative CFO, and decided the system was too risky. Investors demanded that the executive team stop the practice. The result was tragic. The company began a free fall that didn't end until sales had dropped to less than 50% of their peak. In 2009, Arbonne reported sales of just $270 million. Only bankruptcy prevented the company from being ruined by the misstep.

While reasonable minds can disagree on the ethics or risk associated with the sales system employed by Arbonne's field, the critical learning is that the board failed to properly understand and account for the essential role of the sales system. They did not understand that you cannot disrupt or stop a field from using a sales system unless you work with them to replace it with another equally effective one. Without exception, when a sales system is stopped and no thought is given to its replacement, sales begin to decline rapidly.

INNOVATING THE CUSTOMER ACQUISITION SYSTEM

Often a company can experience slowed growth and declining field participation because they have failed to innovate and help the field discover a new customer acquisition system. Perfectly good systems can become outdated and need to be replaced for two reasons:

- Field Fatigue
- Social Media/Technology Changes

Field Fatigue

Unlike a manufacturing system that can be deployed and kept in place for decades with only the need for maintenance from time to time, the systems used in direct selling depend on human beings who get fatigued even if the system is working. During my tenure at Beachbody, weight loss "challenges" became popular and Beachbody, AdvoCare, ViSalus and others built very successful customer acquisition systems around them and grew by hundreds of millions of dollars. By the time I joined AdvoCare, "challenges" still worked, but the field leaders were tired of deploying them and were in desperate need of a new system. In other words, there was still confidence in the products, but the field was tired of doing the same thing year after year and the customer acquisition system was in need of an update. As we began to bring freshness to the customer acquisition system, we began to see renewed energy and participation in the field.

Social Media/Technology Changes

As Facebook moved off of college campuses to become a main street social connection tool, several direct selling companies learned how to do business very effectively on the platform. Younique, Jamberry, Beachbody, and many others saw rapid growth as their field leaders acquired customers on Facebook. While Facebook is still the largest social media platform in terms of total usage, the growth of users and commerce has been migrating to Instagram and YouTube, and few direct sellers have figured out how to adapt or augment their customer acquisitions to these new platforms. Clearly, one of the biggest innovation opportunities awaiting direct sellers is to help distributors identify a system for acquiring customers on new social platforms.

WHERE TO FIND SYSTEMS

Creating customer acquisition systems (or any of the identified systems) is most often a process of discovery rather than of creation. For companies that have sales and thousands of sellers, the process of identifying a new customer acquisition system that can serve as a catalyst for renewed growth begins by identifying those individuals and teams who are growing.

During my tenure at Beachbody, I recognized early on that the company's early growth had not come from traditional recruiting and selling activities but from the identification of founding leaders who brought with them some experienced direct sellers who were close to them. The rest of the growth came as a result of leads the company curated for its distributors from its television direct marketing campaigns. Beachbody sold its fitness programs via infomercial and then assigned all of the customers who were upsold nutritionals by their tele-sales department to their "distributors." In my interviews with top leaders I heard stories of receiving checks without knowing how they were earned. When the company discontinued the aggressive lead program, sales in Team Beachbody (their direct sales division) plummeted from a $50 mm+ run rate to a $36 mm run rate.

After traveling to meet with every top leader, I began to study the financial results and noticed that many of the top sellers were using social media despite our sales team's strong opposition to that practice. I reached out to those top sellers and told them of my interest in learning from them and invited them to the office for a few days of dialogue. I invited each of these sellers to stand and share with the others what they were doing and what they had learned, and allowed the others to ask questions. I sat in the back of the room feverishly taking notes and chimed in with my own questions from time to time. Some of the sellers were more open than others. Most came with concern that the company had called them in to punish them. All left that event having created new allies and having learned from each other. I left the gathering knowing that I had to:

- Choose a System That Could Be Duplicated and Scaled
- Develop a Method of Testing and Refining the System
- Figure Out How to Align the Field Around the New System

Below I will share what I've learned and my advice for identifying new systems to support and scale.

Choosing a System That Can Be Duplicated and Scaled

As you begin to study the individuals and teams who are having success while the majority of your company is struggling, it will become clear which ones understand and use systems and which ones are just extraordinary salespersons.

Throughout my career I had heard over and over again how important people were to success in business. Expert after expert taught that the most successful companies are those that find and enable the best people. Then I read Michael Gerber's account of the founding of McDonald's in his book *The E-Myth Revisited* and my paradigm for direct selling changed forever. Gerber wrote that McDonald's founders Richard and Maurice McDonald realized that they could not attract excellent workers to help them in their restaurant and therefore redesigned their operations to allow below-average employees to produce consistently high-quality products. Ray Kroc eventually discovered the brilliance of that philosophy and the rest is history.

Too many direct selling companies focus on great products, excellent compensation systems and eye-popping marketing and neglect the difficult work of making their customer acquisition system something that is simple enough to ensure the success of below-average distributors. Don't take your eye off my point by assuming I'm encouraging you to ignore great people or to not even aspire to have great people. That is not the point. The point is that you need systems that great people can blow up, but that below-average people can also use to run a profitable business.

As you study the success of those who are growing their business, your primary objective is to separate success that is the result of a great or extraordinary person from success that is a result of an extraordinary and simple system. You are looking for systems, not people, because you can plug anyone into a great system and they will succeed. You can scale with systems faster than you can scale with people.

You can plug anyone into a great system and they will succeed. Therefore, you can scale with great systems faster than you can scale with great people.

Your first goal in finding a system you can scale is to sort through those already being used in your company and separate the system from the salesperson.

It is possible that there are no effective systems, and, in that case, you will be forced to create your own. You should be able to find best practices from multiple people and piece them together into a system. If that is the case for you, I would start by asking—and using experimentation and actual human-to-human experience—to answer the following questions:

- How does one start a discussion about our products with a potential customer? What are the exact words that come out of the seller's mouth? Are they starting from scratch or putting themselves in front of someone who is already looking for your solution? Systems that fail to give sellers the words to use to start a dialogue only work with great conversationalists and fail the "below-average person" test.
- How does one prepare someone to receive an invitation

to purchase or try your product? What are the words of the invitation? How do you bundle the invitation with an offer so compelling that the invitation is more likely to be acted upon?

Here are a few examples of the most effective customer acquisition systems:

- *Arbonne International's "Try this" System*—Arbonne's sellers were taught to drop off their entire line of skincare products with a prospect and say, "I think you are going to love what this skincare does for you and I'm so confident I'm going to let you try the entire line for one week. After a week, I'm going to come by and if you love it, I'll pick up a check. If you don't love it, I'll pick-up the product."
- *Beachbody, AdvoCare, ViSalus's "Weight Loss Challenge"*—"If you're ready to lose weight, come join our accountability group. We are going to help each other earn the prizes our company is offering as part of its challenge."
- *Younique's "Social Video Demonstrations"*—"Don't take my word for it, look at all the customers who are having noticeable results from our product."
- *Beachbody's "See for Yourself Results"*—"Look at all of the people who are losing weight as a result of my coaching. If you want to lose weight, come join my team and I'll get you started with the most compelling starter pack!"
- *Nu Skin's "Before and After Teeth Whitening"*—"Here are my before and after pictures. After using this toothpaste for X days, my teeth are whiter. If you want whiter teeth, DM me."
- *AdvoCare's "Spark Me!"*—"If you are feeling tired every day and don't seem to have the energy to make it through your afternoon, call me and I'll give you a FREE three-day sample of Spark. Don't take my word for it, try it and see for yourself."

- *MONAT Global's "Meet MONAT"*—"Join us for a meetup at (wine bar, bistro). If you have been looking for a great hair care line or a network marketing opportunity, then join me!"

As you can see, great systems are bold and simple. The easiest to duplicate focus on a specific verifiable product benefit. Notice that I'm focused on customer acquisition systems here. Although there are examples of companies that grew primarily with a distributor acquisition system, I believe those days are behind us. While a company needs a great opportunity, the most successful are leading with customer acquisition and then have in place a system for identifying and upgrading their most fanatical customers.

Develop a Method of Testing and Refining the System

Unless your founder is a former distributor who had documented and recent success with systems similar to the one you are advocating, most field leaders are understandably skeptical of any selling systems that come from the company. I am among the corporate executives who have been guilty of being arrogant enough to believe I could create and teach field leaders "how to sell" even though I had never sold anything myself. My experience has taught me that when it comes to creating new sales systems, there is no substitute for testing and validation.

Once you have found, refined or created a customer acquisition system to accompany your current product line or a new product line you plan to introduce, you need to find a way to validate that your system works in practice. It is very challenging to test a new system if it is being designed for a new product that you don't want to preannounce. Your only option is to find employees or hire previous sellers as consultants to test your theory in real world focus groups. Early in my career, I worked with a large consumer packaged goods company that was experimenting with the idea of selling a new home-delivery food line via direct selling. In this case, we hired a former direct seller and used family and friends of corporate executives to test our theories in several markets. While these tests aren't 100% reliable, they are directionally helpful.

Most of the time you will be working on updating or introducing a customer acquisition system designed to work with existing products. I believe the best way to validate these systems is to work with leaders who don't have a strong commitment to their own system, are loyal to the company, are willing to trial the system as you've designed it and then work with you to improve it as necessary. Ideally you want leaders who:

- *Are respected by other leaders*—they can help you sell the system to others if it works.
- *Are actively working*—you want leaders who will deploy your system often, not just once or twice.
- *Are collaborative by nature*—you want leaders who will deploy your system as it was designed (not as they think it should be designed) and then work to improve it from there.
- *Can be trusted to keep secrets*—eventually you will want the world to know about systems that work, but you don't want someone who will erode confidence by sharing the inevitable failures you may experience during your testing.

Align the Field Around Your New System

Once you have validated the effectiveness of your new system you will want to introduce it and convince the majority of your field leaders to migrate from the systems they are using to yours. In my experience, it is not reasonable to believe that ALL leaders will migrate and support the new system. I also do not advocate forcing or coercing them to do so. Instead I've found that the best systems eventually sell themselves. Therefore, my approach to implementing new systems is to delay a large reveal and instead slowly expand your test... first as a beta limited to only those teams who will deploy it by giving it their full support. The ideal introduction will take time and will be more of a "pull" than a "push" strategy. As leaders in your beta begin to have success and talk about it, others who are struggling will want to learn how they can deploy the system on their team. Ideally, the system will be old news and the field will be begging for it by the time it is officially introduced.

Have you heard the saying "go slow to go fast"? In my opinion the fastest way to gain adoption is to introduce it slowly and only as others are demanding it.

During the period of alignment, you will have leaders who will criticize the system or argue that there doesn't need to be a single way of acquiring customers. This is true, and I believe you can and should verbally support systems taught by successful teams. But you should focus your corporate resources on supporting the system you have introduced if it is delivering results. There are tremendous operational efficiencies and real cash savings when the company commits to supporting a single system.

As we committed to the Challenge system at Beachbody, the company began to align its marketing, new product cadence, and sales incentives. We introduced monthly and annual sales incentives that rewarded success in working the system. We avoided wasted spend on marketing programs and sales promotions that did not work. New products were introduced at predictable intervals that supported both seasonal interest in weight loss and the natural timing built into the selling system. New fitness programs were launched as part of a "Challenge Pack" bundle that included the same component parts (no new training!) and priced at one of three predictable price-points, all delivering great value to customers and a strong retail commission for the selling Coach.

It was a great system because everybody knew it, everybody did it, and it worked. This new system became an engine of renewed growth because it required almost no training. Coaches had a "copy and paste" system to follow to achieve sales.

With the customer acquisition system in place, we were able to create a simple coach recruiting system (or Customer to Coach Upgrade System). Recruiting new Coaches became simple. Coaches were taught to listen for customers who talked about being asked if they'd lost weight and were given language to turn those conversations into recruiting opportunities with the simple question, "Have you ever thought of doing what I do?"

Our on-boarding system was simple to create because most of our new Coaches had been part of a Challenge Group and our training staff knew exactly what we wanted new Coaches to do. Our system for getting to profitability was easy because we engineered the economics of our Challenge Packs to benefit those working our system and we could easily show the profitability of following it.

Aligning around a customer acquisition system is not simple. It takes hard work and I don't think it can be done in less than 18 months, but your company can experience growth as the system is perfected and introduced. Whatever the cost in trial, error and patience, the end result is so powerful for a company and its field. I believe there is no better way for a company to spend its time during a period of Renewal. With the exception of a historically few unicorn new products, in my opinion there is no innovation that can improve results faster than to align around a powerful customer acquisition system.

ADVICE FOR FIELD LEADERS

Field Leaders and Systems

While this chapter was written to corporate executives, it is perhaps more relevant to field leaders who more often than not are the source of system innovation. Because you are closer to the customers and new distributors and are selling yourself, you will have much more experience and data to bring to bear when creating new systems. Rather than repeat the information above, let me point out a few common mistakes field leaders make when it comes to systems:

- *Waiting for Corporate*—If your corporate team doesn't have a system, isn't working on one, or has one that is out of touch with reality, you are in the majority. Don't wait for your company to figure things out. Push forward and begin experimenting with systems until you find those that work for your team.
- *You're Not a Good Proxy for What Works*—Notice I said to experiment until you find a system that works for your *team* and not for you. If you are a field leader, chances are you are extraordinary and therefore what works for you probably won't work for most of your team. Remember that your goal is to empower the least skilled member of your team. Great systems make below-average people successful.
- *Allowing the Best to Be Enemy of "Good Enough"*—Someday you may evolve and have the best system, but your team needs systems that are good enough first because chances are they will do nothing (or very little) unless you give them something that shows them what to do.
- *Keeping Your System or the Process "Confidential"*—When developing systems you want as many good people involved as possible. Just because someone is crossline doesn't mean they shouldn't be involved. Find crossline leaders to work with. Split the load and have one person focus on one system (customer acquisition) while the other focuses on another (upgrading customers to distributors). The power of systems is truly experienced when "everyone is doing it" and the company doesn't have to choose an organization to support.

RENEWAL

CHAPTER 9: PRODUCT INNOVATION—
Evolutionary or Revolutionary?

"If you see my new product but don't buy it, that's my failure, not yours."

— SETH GODIN, MARKETING CONSULTANT

We've given most of our innovation attention to the importance of selling systems. In this chapter we will turn our attention to new products. While new products play a very important role in jump-starting or continuing the growth of direct selling companies, not all new products play an equally important role. Some selling systems are more dependent on new products than others. Understanding the role of new products in your company's selling system and being clear about the type of new product you are introducing will help you make the most of any new product introduction.

One important reminder: new products consume cash. In a world where cash is scarce, new products can be the single biggest consumer of cash. That's why making sure that your new product results in new sales is critical… but not a sure bet.

NEW PRODUCTS MUST FIT THE CUSTOMER ACQUISITION SYSTEM

New products are often thought of as the key driver to increase growth. However, great direct selling companies understand the customer acquisition system being used by their distributors and make sure new products don't disrupt that system. Great companies work with field leaders to ensure that the products are introduced with an accompanying sales system. Or, they deliberately teach distributors to continue to focus on the "lead story" and how to use the new product as a follow-on opportunity for existing customers or for prospects that don't respond to the lead.

For example, catalog companies like Avon, Home Interiors, Pampered Chef and Thirty-One Gifts rely on innovative and seasonal products to give customers a reason to return to a party or to look through their most recent catalog. Executives from these companies will argue that managing their product pipeline is one of their most important responsibilities. However, most network marketing companies rely on a hero product and it's likely their customer acquisition system is built around that single product. Companies with hero products or with product packs focused on a single benefit (e.g. weight loss) struggle to effectively use new products.

I learned this lesson early in my career at USANA Health Sciences where we had a sales force that was leading with our core vitamin and mineral product, the Essentials. Our founder was a scientist and the story told by our distributors all led to the Essentials. However, a majority of the management team became convinced that we needed a skin care line, so we launched a very good line with a tie-in to the company's science-based founding. The line initially sold out as current distributors and customers ordered the product to sample it for themselves and their families. To make sure we could keep up with demand we acquired a manufacturer to make the product for us. In the end, it never grew beyond the current base and never became a significant seller. In fact, the entire line made up less than 10% of sales and the field struggled to find any new customers for any of our products until they decided to ignore the new skin care line and go back to telling the story they knew about the Essentials.

A similar thing happened to AdvoCare just before I joined the company. They introduced a "Fit" line with great data to support that the "Weekend Warrior" target market was robust and growing.

Unfortunately, AdvoCare's sales force had effectively grown using a customer acquisition system focused on weight loss. They knew how to use weight loss products to acquire new customers and didn't have a system to acquire Weekend Warriors. With no system in place to sell this new line, the distributors purchased it for their own use, recommended it from time to time, and continued to struggle. Within weeks of joining the company, we refocused our time and attention on weight loss, renewed our weight loss-based customer acquisition system and began to see our topline slowly but surely improve for the first time in three years.

These two companies are not alone. Younique tried to build on the launch of a fragrance line despite the fact that their presenters ("presenters" being the title Younique uses for its distributors) knew how to use mascara to acquire new customers. Longaberger tried to launch jewelry despite the fact that their distributors knew how to sell home décor and specifically, baskets. Company after company pulls out their product innovation playbook and launches what they believe will be a transformational new product line only to disappoint their field and their factories.

Product innovation without proper consideration for the customer acquisition needed to sell a new product is a recipe for failure... not only failure to meet expectations but also continued failure to renew growth. The good news is that companies that understand the significance of systems will recognize the opportunity they have to effectively innovate both their systems and the products supported by them.

The choices for innovation then include:

- Innovate products that fit the current customer acquisition system.

- Innovate and refresh the current customer acquisition system with little or no change to the products, or
- Innovate a new customer acquisition system to support a blockbuster new product.

FINDING NEW PRODUCTS THAT FIT THE CURRENT SYSTEM

Having experienced hockey stick growth and serious declines over the years, Nu Skin broke with the industry's tradition of introducing new products as a "surprise." During his tenure as CEO of Nu Skin, Truman Hunt threw out the long-standing practice of keeping all new products as closely guarded secrets and developed a thorough process for allowing qualifying leaders to respond to new product ideas years before they would be launched. These leaders understood the field's selling systems and knew how to prepare for and adapt them to make the most of new products without disrupting the systems. To date, Nu Skin is one of the only companies to practice this collaborative method of new product development with its associated multi-year lead time, and to their credit, they have seen incremental sales from new product introductions. The system they use today has been adapted over the years, but they have pioneered a process of collaboration that other companies would do well to learn from and employ.

When I've shared this story with other CEOs most of them will say, "We do that with our leaders." Further discussion reveals that the key difference is not whether top leaders receive a "preview" before new products are launched, but whether or not that preview happens early enough in the process to meaningfully influence whether or how that new product is launched. Nu Skin's process starts years in advance while most of my colleagues are previewing product weeks or days in advance. By then, little can be done to stop, change or even modify the product or its launch plan.

The best companies work hand-in-hand with their field leaders to create a unified marketing and sharing system that makes it easy for the field and leaves new reps thinking, "I can do that" and leaves company management crystal clear in their understanding of how to deploy company resources to support that system. Today, far too many companies leave the selling system to their independent distributors.

NEW PRODUCTS IN TODAY'S DIRECT SELLING COMPANY

Amway has been a trailblazer in the direct selling channel for many years. In the early 90s when I first joined Melaleuca, Inc., Amway clearly considered itself a distribution channel and as such introduced almost every imaginable product and service. In those days, company after company would approach direct sellers asking them to offer credit cards, phone service, travel and other discount programs to sell to their distributors. These experiments lasted for just a few years and direct sellers began to realize that while their distributors wanted new products, they couldn't effectively sell or often wouldn't buy products and services they didn't see as a core competency of the company. The theory of direct sellers as a channel of distribution died and has evolved to recognize that direct selling companies are brands, their distributors are extensions of their brand and the basic rules of brand extension must be applied in their strictest form. Plugging off-brand products into a company doesn't work, but introducing new and/or improved products can be value creating.

The value of new products is primarily dependent on the type of direct seller promoting it. For example, most consumable companies have a hero product sold to customers and distributors via a subscription model. Rarely will a new product gain enough attention and traction to become a meaningful and incremental part of these companies' sales. However, companies that rely on catalog, party or VIP sales with little "same SKU sales" and a dependence on more "same customer sales" need a consistent stream of compelling products. For these companies, new products are essential and can make or break their future.

NEW PRODUCTS IN CONSUMABLE COMPANIES

When I first arrived at USANA, the company was following the industry norm of relying on quarterly events and new product launches at those events to drive excitement and growth. It didn't take long for me to realize that our product line was expanding faster than our revenue line. New product plans always predicted incremental sales but rarely produced any noticeable change in average order size or frequency. What we learned at USANA, and what has since become more widely known among consumable product companies, is that new products do not lead to more sales, only increased costs and less cash available for investment.

Here are some of the ways we effectively weaned our field from their expectation of new products and systematized new products to avoid disruption:

- *Substituted "News" for New Products*—At USANA we began to experiment with releasing "news" rather than new products and found that an announcement of a partnership, sponsorship or new program was as motivating as a new product announcement... and much less expensive.
- *Reformulated and Improved Existing Products*—We applied our valuable learnings and began to reformulate products rather than creating new ones. We even eliminated SKUs by combining a few products, delivering great value to our consumers and significant profit improvements for the company.
- *Created Easy-to-Substitute Bundles*—At Beachbody, we effectively increased the lifetime value of customers by creating bundles that followed the same value proposition and were all built on our hero product (Shakeology). We sold new fitness programs in a bundle with Shakeology as a subscription. These bundles all fit the same price points, had the same rewards and commissions for distributors, and offered a great value for our

customers. In essence, distributors were selling and reselling one SKU—a challenge pack—that had enough variety to keep their customers coming back for more.

NON-SUBSCRIPTION COMPANIES NEED A STRONG PRODUCT PIPELINE

A strong product pipeline is particularly important to those companies that do not have a consumable product. For example, fashion, home decor, kitchen utilities and home furnishing companies all live and die on the quality of their new products and the soundness of thinking around frequency, launch communication, pricing and positioning. Companies will give thought to the frequency with which their customers want to be sold to, and this may depend on what is required of them. Customers who must attend a party to be introduced to new products will have high expectations of the quality of "new" they will see, versus customers who are part of a Facebook VIP group and casually drop in to see what is new.

Great person-to-person selling companies train their distributors and employees to understand how new products are used to create new selling experiences. They have clarity around the "customer reorder system" they are supporting (Facebook VIP, party, etc.) and make sure their cadence and new products effectively empower that resell experience. They ensure that distributors understand and plan their business around the cadence and use of new products.

NEW PRODUCT CADENCE

It wasn't until my tenure as head of Beachbody's network marketing company that I would fully appreciate the last important part of a new product plan: the cadence or timing of new product introductions. When I arrived at Beachbody, they had planned new product launches around seasonal interest in weight loss, adjusted slightly to account for television inventory (the company's primary revenues came from their infomercial business at the time). As the growth of the network marketing division accelerated and it became clear that it would be our future, we rethought the cadence and came up with a predictable pattern of product launches and promotions. The predictability and pattern created operational efficiencies in the company, but its real impact came in the field as our part-time sellers learned how to prepare and maximize each promotion and new product. Our growth continued to accelerate.

Later in my career I had the chance to work with one of our channel's great companies. This organization had fallen into the habit of using new product launches and promotions to continue their growth. They were clearly in the Growth by Promotion stage of their business lifecycle. The lack of a pattern in any of their data and the randomness of their new product launches showed how unpredictable their business had become. The company was introducing dozens of SKUs every quarter and while they could point to a slowing but growing topline, they didn't notice the impact their activity was having on sponsoring, which had slowed to a crawl. It took someone with a fresh set of eyes to help them see that their field leaders had gone from 90% sponsoring to 90% responding to and trying to make the most of new product launches and promotions.

Just as a predictable new product cadence can free the field to improve the effectiveness of each launch, new products introduced in a seemingly random but frequent pattern can disrupt the field entirely and make it virtually impossible for field leaders to do anything other than respond to company stimulus.

I mentioned Nu Skin earlier but I failed to share one of the most interesting lessons I learned from them, and that was how to use new product launches to drive sponsoring and advancements. One of the results of their pattern of involving leaders progressively in launch plans and then pre-announcing the date a new product will be launched is that leaders can actually begin to use that information as a tool in their sponsoring. Nu Skin's new product "pre-launches" would generate so much volume in such a short period of time that leaders would recruit to the promise of being able to benefit from a pre-launch. The actual launch of these products a year after the pre-launch may have been similar to the non-incremental results of most consumable companies, but the pre-launch was purely incremental, and leaders turned it into something significantly beneficial by sponsoring new distributors in anticipation of every new pre-launch.

IS YOUR NEW PRODUCT REVOLUTIONARY OR EVOLUTIONARY?

For the most part, sellers want to avoid disappointing corporate executives. If the company sets an expectation for a product, they want to meet that expectation. However, often companies will launch what is essentially a good product line extension—an evolutionary product—in a way that makes the field believe the product is a unicorn that deserves all of their time and attention now... a revolutionary product.

If I were running a direct selling company today, I would review every new product proposal to first determine if the product is revolutionary or evolutionary. Evolutionary products can be slotted into the product plan with clear instruction to the field on how it complements the current customer acquisition system, which should be built around a hero product. In other words, I would make sure the field doesn't lead with the evolutionary new product, but instead uses it to try and generate additional sales from current customers while they continue to acquire new ones with the hero product.

If a product has the potential of becoming a new hero, I would task the sales team to not only focus innovation around the product but also around the system for selling it. I would never launch a potential hero without having a clear and tested customer acquisition system for it, and I would only launch a second hero if I was confident my first hero had outlived its useful life. Having two heroes on the field at the same time is like having two quarterbacks. It is not impossible, but there is not a lot of data to show that it can work as effectively as focusing does.

SUMMARY OF PRODUCT INNOVATION LEARNING

A thoughtful product strategy means that proper consideration has been given to your brand and how new products will fit into its current customer acquisition system. The most successful companies will distinguish between revolutionary products that need a customer acquisition system and those that are evolutionary and make sure the field is clear on how you expect the new product to help them. Finally, give thought to an appropriate new product cadence. Allow your field leaders to anticipate and plan for new product launches rather than leaving them to respond to surprises spaced haphazardly throughout the year.

A FEW LAST THOUGHTS ON PRODUCT INNOVATION

What about when a blockbuster product sells out? There are several amazing examples of how sudden demand for existing products or response to new products have completely changed the trajectory of direct selling companies. For example:

- *SeneGence*—had a distributor figure out how to demonstrate the durability of their lipstick and a company with steady sales experienced Hyper-Growth overnight.
- *Nu Skin*—a new distributor figured out how to use before and after pictures to sell their ten-year-old whitening toothpaste. The product flew off the shelves and the company experienced renewed growth in North America.
- *LuLaRoe*—figured out how to sell stretchy pants with unique patterns and couldn't keep them in stock.
- *Younique*—launched 3D and years later 4D mascara and sold out on multiple occasions despite "aggressive" forecasting.
- *Origami Owl*—had to use a waiting list to accommodate demand from new distributors when the story of Bella Weems' new

locket jewelry went viral.

If you are fortunate to find a product that you can't keep in stock, don't despair. Rejoice in your good fortune, communicate clearly with your field and make sure to tell the world. There is nothing like true, unplanned scarcity to drive growth and companies that do their best to meet demand and spend time adjusting their core customer acquisition system around their new blockbuster product usually win. Be careful not to assume you have your new customer acquisition system just because you have more customers than you need. Scarcity is a great growth driver, but its utility is, well... scarce. When the scarcity is gone, if your field has only learned how to use scarcity to attract others, your growth will dry up immediately. Great products can grow sales, but only when coupled with a great system can it sustain them.

ADVICE FOR FIELD LEADERS
How Field Leaders Should Use New Products

Field leaders need to have their own clarity around how new products fit into their team's selling system. Leaders need to recognize when a product is *evolutionary* and should be sold to existing customers as follow-on purchase options and when a product is *revolutionary* and needs its own customer acquisition system. This decision is critical and requires decisiveness because a team with two customer acquisition systems is no better off than a team with none. Here are my suggestions for field leaders:

- *Don't Let Your Team Get Distracted by a New Product or Product Line*—If your team is selling weight loss and you're given a weight training product don't let your team stop selling weight loss to start selling this new product. Teach them how to offer it to existing customers (hopefully you have a system for that) and then refocus your team on the customer acquisition system that is working.

- *Recognize Revolutionary Products and Pivot*—If your company does come out with a new product that is much better or easier to sell than others, take the time to create a customer acquisition system to sell the new product and teach your team to pivot to the new system (not to add the new system). Great growth comes when teams have a single customer acquisition system and, if necessary, a system for upselling other products to existing customers.
- *Create a System for Selling Non-Hero Products*—Hero products are those that you build your customer acquisition system around. It can be one product or a product bundle, but it's not "all products." If your team has learned to acquire customers with a hero product and your company continues to introduce more and more products, you need a system for selling these new products to existing customers so your team doesn't try and use these new products to acquire new customers. I've seen far too many distributors stop growing because they were trying to sell non-hero products to new customers. Field leaders owe it to their team to make it super clear which product(s) they acquire customers with and which products they sell to existing customers.

CHAPTER 10: COMPENSATION INNOVATION—

Rewarding Growth with the Right Incentives

"People work for money but go the extra mile for recognition, praise and rewards."

— DALE CARNEGIE, LEADERSHIP TRAINER

N

When it comes to motivating others to sell more and sponsor more leaders, the first thought that comes to mind is often rewards and compensation: pulling together a sales contest, offering a new incentive for growing a team or even looking at a complete overhaul of the compensation system. In this chapter we will discuss how and when to consider compensation plan changes and how to use other short-term incentives instead of plan changes or to test a change prior to implementation.

In conversations with founders of direct selling companies, I often hear them talk about two aspects of their business: (1) their products, and (2) their compensation plan. Never do I hear founders talk about how they are going to acquire customers or about their system for upgrading customers to distributors. Many founders seem to believe that if they have great products and a compensation plan like Company Y that has been successful, then they too will have success and their distributors will figure out how to sell the products. That's not always the case.

COMPENSATION PLAN DESIGN

I am not an expert in direct selling compensation plans, but I have expertly employed elements of compensation to create huge growth for companies. I believe that the ideal is to design your compensation plan last, not first, and to make sure that it is designed to promote the behaviors required to make your selling systems work. The wise founder will first develop a sellable product, then design a system of introducing it to customers, then convince customers to both buy and use the product, and then create follow-on systems to upgrade that customer to a distributor, to onboard the distributor, to create a profitable business, etc., etc. Once such a system is in place, a compensation is designed to reward the activities of the system. The ideal looks much like the diagram below:

Product → **Selling System** → **Compensation Plan**

The ideal compensation system will be built with consideration given to the FTC's most recent guidelines (see my notes at the end of this chapter for the latest FTC guidelines at the time this book was first published), and will have the proper mix of money devoted to selling vs. building and leading a team. A great compensation plan will also have a wise mix of money focused on growth activities (those results that actually produce results today) and residual money.

If you or I were to retire tomorrow, we would expect that even a generous retirement program would compensate us less than we would make if we continued to go to work every day. Yet too many compensation systems are balanced so heavily toward paying leaders large residuals for building teams that they can retire on those residuals and stop performing behaviors that help grow the business. Even though they've stopped leading and motivating a team, their compensation doesn't go down and in some cases, it increases. While this model might work during Hyper-Growth, companies that have survived to see their distributors reach retirement age have found that they no longer have money in their compensation plan to fund new leader growth. They are left to stand by and watch helplessly as their business is held hostage by their legacy leaders. For that reason, I believe it is a mistake to have more than 30-40% of your core compensation system rewarding retirement activities.

Finally, I think that great companies never change their compensation plan, or if they do, they make only infrequent and minor tweaks rather than wholesale changes. The list of companies that have found Renewal with a new compensation plan is likely very short. Changing the core compensation plan is so disruptive to a company that I am a proponent of having very strong annual and monthly incentive programs that focus the field on growth activities and give the company the opportunity to adjust the rules and requirements annually to meet current business needs. Later in this chapter we will discuss my preferred model for short-term incentive programs, but first let's talk about what you should do if you are forced to change your compensation plan because you believe it is not within the FTC's current guidelines, or you have come to realize that the plan you have is not feasible (e.g. you're paying out more than you can afford).

Here are the steps I would take if tasked to lead a compensation plan change for a company:

1. *Design the New Plan to Reward Behavior*—Start by working with a compensation plan consultant who can help you map out the behavior you need to reward to sell your product and grow your business and to make sure your plan has all of the features necessary to not only sell but also to sponsor and lead teams.
2. *Model Your New Plan*—Most compensation plan consultants can use your current data to model the impact of your plan. It will be tough to predict how it will change behavior in a mathematical model, but at the very least you can answer

the question: "If this plan had been in place in the last 12-18 months, how would have it impacted our current distributors?"

I ask for data to be given to me so that I can focus in on the biggest winners (those who would have made significantly more as a result of the change) and the biggest losers (those who would have lost the most because of the change). I then work with corporate sales staff to answer the question: "Is this plan rewarding the right people?" In other words, have I redistributed my compensation dollars to more accurately match the results actually being produced by my distributors? If I have, then I can move forward to the next step. If I haven't, I continue to make modifications to the plan.

3. *Develop a Transition Plan*—Often a plan will have such a significant impact on the field that they will need time to adjust their activity to minimize the impact on their earnings. Remember that many distributors have made life decisions (mortgages, left full-time jobs, etc.) based on the income they are earning from your current plan. You will want to consider announcing the plan and giving the distributors time to prepare for the change or to create short-term incentives to bridge legacy distributors for a time.

4. *Engage Your Team in Communicating and Launching*—While I don't think it is wise to allow a few distributors to help you design a new compensation system (it is too difficult to avoid the human tendency to design a plan that favors your own self-interests), I do believe it's critical to bring field leaders into your planning process before the new plan is launched. These leaders can help you assess how much of an impact the plan will have, and as you educate them, they can help you craft the best strategy for communicating and launching the plan to the

rest of the field.

While the proper use of rewards and incentives can be especially helpful and should be part of the innovation work you do with your team, I caution against starting with compensation and incentives.

WHEN INCENTIVES PUNISH MORE THAN THEY REWARD

Earlier in my career, I learned that my best laid incentive plans often went awry in one of two ways: (1) The earning thresholds were set at levels that reflected the norms a few months ago, but ended up being unachievable for most given the business's current performance, or (2) it presupposed that leaders needed a new incentive to sell or sponsor when in fact they didn't need motivation but education—or a new selling system, because what had worked in the past was no longer working. In other words, selling systems can become ineffectual and you end up with distributors who are doing the "same old thing" without the "same old results." Fix the system and help distributors adjust to new norms with a process that leads to renewed performance and growth. Without a new way of acquiring customers, all the incentives in the world will have little lasting impact on renewing growth.

Sometimes the problem has nothing to do with compensation or systems, but the company's product is just not compelling. If your distributors are having a hard time getting reorders, it's time to focus efforts on improving your product(s).

Touch the compensation plan last—unless you need to bring it current with today's regulatory environment. Instead, I have found the most success in focusing on short-term incentives that use points, prizes and vacations to move the field.

CREATING A CONTEST CURRENCY

I have found that one of the most valuable tools a company can create for itself is that of a contest currency, typically in the form of points that can be used to reward behaviors your compensation plan doesn't specifically reward, or to reward the results you know you need in order to grow. One of my clients was implementing a direct selling model on top of their current franchise model and didn't want to have multilevel compensation to reward sellers for recruiting other sellers (that was the role of the franchise owner). Instead of creating another layer of compensation, the company used its annual incentive program and the points used to qualify for that incentive as the currency to reward referrals of other sellers (they had a simple program to allow sellers to earn matching contest points on anyone they referred to the company who became a new seller).

I have found that great short-term incentives have the following elements:

- *Contest Currency*—Points used to track and gamify progress.
- *Monthly (or Weekly) Prizes*—Create something that rewards immediate activity (especially helpful as a means of motivating new sellers to produce volume in their first few weeks/months). Early in my career I discovered that you never want to leave achievers guessing as to the definition of success. Tell them by establishing a monthly hurdle: sell X number of products or Y dollars' worth of products to Z new customers and you will have achieved success. The simple act of defining success empowers achievers and creates fuel to ignite growth from thin air.

The simple act of defining success empowers achievers and creates fuel to ignite growth from thin air.

I have found that small prizes like shirts, bags, balls, etc. can be as effective at motivating behavior as large cash incentives. Sometimes a leader board and weekly/monthly recognition of the top sellers in a time period is sufficient to obtain the desired behavior. Mary Kay Ash is quoted as saying, "There are two things people want more than sex and money... recognition and praise." Build an incentive program that allows them to earn both and you will start to see growth.

- *Annual Incentives*—Create a plan to reward consistency over a period of time. My preference is to have both an annual point total required to earn the prize and to make it easy by multiplying points to reward consistency. For example, if you set a monthly goal of earning five points, then they could earn multiple their monthly points by two if they meet the goal two months in a row, by three for three consecutive months, etc. You might also consider giving bonus multipliers for points earned during the first few weeks or months for new sellers, so those who join late in the year still have some hope of earning annual recognition.

  Annual incentives are most often vacations, but they could be anything worth working for, even recognition or appointment to a special advisory board. If you can afford a vacation, I like to break up the opportunity of earning into chunks so that someone can earn part of a trip (or a trip for one), then airfare and then a second person and later an upgrade (e.g. to their room or class of air service). The more you tier your programs the more people you will have engaged in the contest later in the year.
- *Keep It Simple*—The easier your contest is to understand the more people you will have participating. You can make your incentives simple by following these three suggestions: (1) have just one or two simple ways of earning points, and (2) keep your rules the same from year to year, and (3) adjust point thresholds annually as necessary.

When you create a contest that is consistent you will be surprised how powerful it can be. At one of my previous companies we created a contest called Success Club. Individuals could make it into the Success Club every month by earning five points (eventually we created a second level called Success Club 10 to give the top achievers more to push for each month). Points were earned when you sold a new customer a challenge pack. If you earned 80 Success Club points or qualified for Success Club for eight months, you would qualify for a trip (with tiers from there). The top Success Club point earner each year was also recognized as the top producer and the top ten producers earned a VIP vacation.

After just a few months of putting this program in place, distributors rarely talked about the company's core compensation plan. All the talk was about Success Club. The relatively small amount of money we spent on this contest arguably drove much more growth than the significant dollars spent on our core compensation plan.

MONEY IS NOT THE BEST MOTIVATOR

I have learned that money is not always the best motivator and have learned from Pollen that it's not always required. Pollen, formerly known as VERVE, has built a $250 million business (at the time of this writing) in the entertainment and travel industry with an independent sales force that doesn't get paid a dime. They earn tickets to events for inviting friends to come along and if they get X friends their experience gets better and better with backstage passes, meet and greet, etc.

We live in a world where everyone wants to show the world what they are experiencing. Tap into the power of recognition and the multiplying power of allowing someone to be recognized publicly (on social media, for example) doing something incredible, and you will find a tool much more powerful than money to fuel your company's growth.

LAYERING INNOVATION

I do believe you can re-ignite growth in a company with the proper incentives but layering your innovation so that you have multiple tools working for you is often the most powerful way to generate momentum. Launching a new product can be powerful, but when you launch it with a new brand, a sampling system that makes it easy to share it and an incentive that rewards those who follow the system, the power of that new product launch is significantly improved.

FTC Guidelines
Notes from presentation made by Andrew Smith, Director FTC 10/8/19

Your Compensation System May Be a Pyramid Scheme if It:
- Is an aggressive recruitment-based compensation system (not just the absence of sales to the end consumer)
- Requires recruiting to recoup the initial expense
- Is mathematically impossible for most of the distributors to achieve even modest earnings without recruiting others.

Questions to ask:

o *Does your program overly incentivize for recruitment rather than product sales?*
  - "Distributors have to recruit to advance to earn certain types of compensation."
  - "Selling product alone will not allow the distributor to qualify for certain promotions and rewards, even if he manages to sell millions of dollars of product."
  - "Individuals who only were able to find some recruits or who were not able to find any recruits made little to no money."

o *Does your program create incentives for distributors to purchase more products than they actually need?*
  - A reward system encourages distributors to buy goods, not to satisfy their own means or inventory to re-sale, but solely to earn bonuses, commissions or other rewards from the scheme.
  - If your average order amount per distributor is about the same as your distributor's monthly sales requirement, that is evidence they are buying to earn, and not for personal use.

o *Does your program encourage or incentivize distributors to make big purchases right up front when they join?*
  - Do the majority of distributors earn enough to recoup their upfront purchase?

Even the perfect refund policy would not [be sufficient] to rebut evidence that distributors are buying products to earn bonuses or meet compensation thresholds. Especially troublesome are policies that require distributors to jump through hoops or resign from the business before being eligible for refunds.

CHAPTER 11: SIMPLIFY—
Removing Layers to Discover the Core

"The art of simplicity is a puzzle of complexity."

— DOUGLAS HORTON, DEAN, HARVARD DIVINITY SCHOOL

When I think of simplicity I think of Apple and its founder Steve Jobs, who said, "That's been one of my mantras— focus and simplicity. Simple can be harder than complex: you have to work hard to get your thinking clean to make it simple. But it's worth it in the end because once you get there, you can move mountains."

While there is not a specific sequence to the C.H.I.S.E.L. formula for Renewal, I believe it will be easier for your company to simplify if you have first gone through the process of determining what you will stop doing in order to meet your cash needs. Also, essential: being clear about your selling systems and the role of innovation in your Renewal plan.

WHAT SIMPLIFYING IS NOT

In most companies I work with, the task of simplifying often generates a long list of things "to do" because the focus turns to simplifying customer interactions rather than simplifying the business itself. For example, most marketing executives can create pages of changes that could be made to the company's website to "simplify" the order process. While that type of project may make the list eventually, the simplification efforts that will make the difference in renewing the company have more to do with what you should *stop* doing than those items that would make a list of what you need to do now.

SIMPLE MEANS FEWER SURPRISES

For most direct selling companies, getting to simple will include answering the question "What should we stop doing?" But that's not all. Mostly it is about making things more predictable for your organization, internally and in the field. In other words, simplicity is less about doing fewer things and more about having fewer surprises.

Simplicity is less about doing fewer things and more about having fewer surprises.

I love to use the analogy of Christmas when I talk about simplicity. Most of us don't want fewer presents at Christmas and most of us want to be surprised Christmas morning, but none of us wants to wake up and suddenly learn that today is Christmas. Surprises are only manageable when those who must act to create the response aren't surprised by the timing or expectation. Companies that randomly surprise field leaders and then expect them to execute and mobilize their teams will eventually wear out their field—even though they are "giving" them great new products that should help them make money. Instead of springing new product launches on your field, create a calendar of new product launch dates and provide your leaders clear expectations and tools to execute with so when they are surprised by "what" you are launching, they are prepared to partner with you and magnify the results with their teams

Simplicity is sometimes not about doing less, but rather about surprising people less.

SIMPLIFYING THE COMPLEXITY OF SIMPLIFYING

As Steve Jobs said in the quote cited earlier, the work of making things simple is so, so difficult and requires WAY more finesse than making things good enough. Simplification will require prior work on strategy and systems and then great discipline and patience in execution. Getting to the point where your field recognizes and acknowledges that you have simplified things for them will take time, but let me give you a framework that will help you jump-start the process. I call it the **Three C's of Simplification:**

- *Calendar*—start with a calendar with a full year published in advance.
- *Cadence*—think carefully about how often your field needs something (new product, promotion, incentive, meetings) and create a consistent cadence. Good businesses have a rhythm their field can clap along with.
- *Communication*—companies that are simple to work with have a consistent communication system and the field knows when, how, and from whom they can expect to hear about specific topics.

Calendar—Publish Your Plan for a Full Year

For the first decade of my career in direct selling this headline would have been like the fast forward button I would have pressed to skip to the next point as soon as possible. Like many direct selling companies, it seemed like the companies I worked for were always operating in response mode. If that sounds like your company, the thought of publishing a calendar a year in advance seems impossible, but it's not. You simply start with what you know and improve your calendar over time.

I learned the power of a calendar from an architect, a soft-spoken, humble man by the name of Bill Nelson who volunteered as my advisor in a church assignment I had in my mid-thirties. I was responsible for overseeing a home-to-home ministering program that paired two members of our church and assigned them to visit and "watch over" a few families. My role was to visit with each of these companionships every quarter to see how their families where doing and to find out if there was anything the church could do to help them. I loved the concept and I had every intent of fulfilling my commitment, but I was a busy executive and traveling all the time. The quarters would fly by before I would get around to meeting with anyone.

Bill was supportive and recognized my desire to serve. He asked if he could make a suggestion and I said "Sure!"

"Why don't you take time now to schedule your four interviews with each companionship for the entire year," he said. "You might end up traveling or they might have something come up, but it will be much easier for you to reschedule than to be constantly scheduling."

I took Bill's advice. It worked like a charm.

I've applied Bill's tactic as an executive in every company I've worked in since that conversation. I know what I want to do (be in the field two to four days every month), which conferences I want to attend, what direct reports I should meet with and how often I want to talk with them, and what "big events" I have at home (anniversary, first day of school, etc.). At the beginning of each year, I put those on my calendar and fill in new details that come along or make revisions as necessary.

You will be surprised at how much you know if you will just sit down, answer the following questions and begin making notations in your calendar:

- When is our annual convention?
- What other field meetings/visits should we schedule (or how often)? Publishing a calendar that simply says "field meetings" in May can be sufficient as a starting point.
- How frequently should we introduce new products and when

do we think those dates will be?
- What promotions do we want to continue or start this year? (e.g. Black Friday, Back-to-School, Valentine's, Mother's Day, etc.).
- When will we communicate (conference calls, emails, newsletters, etc.)?
- When will we introduce or go on our annual incentive trip? (Hint: don't put the location on the calendar if it hasn't been announced. Just say "annual incentive trip.")

Providing your field with a calendar that helps them anticipate and plan for announcements and "surprises" will immediately make things feel more straightforward and will increase morale and excitement. One other advantage: the calendar will also communicate sustainability. As many of you have learned, whenever sales start to decline, people immediately begin to fear the worst—"We are going out of business!" Publishing a calendar is a subtle way of anchoring your field in the future again and helping to offset that negative thinking.

Cadence

I may be the worst dancing partner on the planet and I hung up my baritone after the 8th grade. No one has accused me of being a musician since. But I know enough about dancing and music to understand that great songs are built on a foundation of a clearly defined rhythm. The most excellent dancers, composers and musicians are inspired by the rhythm established at the beginning of a score and often kept by a skilled percussionist.

Publishing a calendar is a terrific way to start the simplification process, but defining a cadence that sets the pace for that calendar is where the magic starts happening.

Each month of our life is made of more than 2.5 million component parts we call seconds. If each of those seconds had a random duration, the amount of mental energy it would take to track our progress would increase significantly and could be the cause of major stress and anxiety. Imagine that you have an appointment at noon but you're not exactly sure if the amount of time you have between the current time (say, 11 am) is going to be the equivalent of 3,600 evenly spaced seconds, or if some of those seconds might be equivalent to five seconds, or if on average the time was equivalent to 60 seconds for each one second. What makes time so valuable and allows it to play such a significant role in our lives (without requiring much brain power) is that it is consistent and predictable.

A study published in 2016 in *Nature Communications* and summarized in *The Guardian* by Marc Lewis found that "uncertainty is even more stressful than knowing something bad is definitely going to happen."[17] When we create uncertainty for our field—even when the uncertainty is intended to be something we think will help their business—we increase our sellers' stress levels and our business becomes complex or difficult for them.

You create cadence in your organization by committing to a pattern of doing business... a pattern of communications. Consistency around when and how often you will launch new products, promotions, or incentives. Uniformity in how and how often you will recognize and reward your sellers and field leaders. For example, a product promotion cadence might mean that you will offer a customer promotion on the first Monday of each month and it will expire on Wednesday that same week. Your calendar would not reveal what that promotion would be, but the fact that its coming can be published. If it happens consistently the same day of the month or every X days/months, then it is part of your business cadence.

A great example of using cadence for incentives is the practice of announcing a leadership incentive every January at a "leaders only" event and an incentive for all sellers at the summer annual convention. Again, the field knows that there will be a new incentive announced twice a year and when and where that announcement will take place,

[17] https://www.theguardian.com/commentisfree/2016/apr/04/uncertainty-stressful-research-neuroscience, accessed November 12, 2019.

but they are surprised by the prize or location of the incentive trip.

Not only does a predictable company cadence reduce the stress levels of your field and make them feel like doing business with you is simple, but companies with a strong cadence will reduce costs associated with constantly rushing to meet short deadlines and the extra headcount added to allow departments to respond to the executive team's latest idea.

Communication

When I joined Origami Owl and had the chance to listen to leaders for the first time, I was surprised to hear them express their disappointment in the company's poor communication. I was surprised because I knew the company was engaging multiple channels of communication and it felt like we were communicating all the time.

As I pushed these leaders to try to better understand their concerns, it became clear that it wasn't the *quantity* of communication that was the problem but the lack of a communication cadence. The field didn't necessarily need more information, but they were always afraid that they would miss something. In other words, we might launch a new program on our Facebook page one week and announce a new product on our YouTube channel the next. Leaders wanted to know exactly when and where to tune in for each type of communication. They didn't want to be responsible for monitoring every channel the company was using.

Companies should have a communication system that includes a cadence or frequency of communication. A great communication system starts by answering the questions:

1. *"What do we communicate to the field?"* Things like training, inspirational stories, policy changes, new products, promotions, advancements and recognition, etc.
2. *"Who do we communicate with?"* You will find that some

information is suitable for general release, some should be communicated first to field leaders and then from them to their teams, and other information is better communicated only to leaders. Getting clarity about the type of information that goes to your separate audiences and building a plan for each audience is best practice.

3. *"When and how frequently should we communicate?"* Again, this question could be broken down by content (examples listed above) but should also have built in "opportunity." For example, one of Walmart's competitive advantages is a shift meeting they hold for employees of each department at the beginning of each shift. Walmart doesn't always have critical content to share in the shift meetings every day, yet the meetings have become an advantage because when they do have time sensitive information to relay, they already have a mechanism in place to ensure all employees receive it from a trusted source within 24 hours.

So, as you plan your cadence with your field, make sure you build in some flexibility and have a mechanism in place that allows you a method of communicating with them on short notice.

4. *"What channel will you use to communicate?"* We have so many options for communication today. From video conferencing to text messaging to good old-fashioned telephone conferencing to newsletters... you'll find that your field has preferences. You might choose different channels for different messages and that might be driven in part by the audience (e.g. senior leaders vs. all sellers). Whichever channel you choose is important, but even more important is to be consistent in using that channel to communicate specific types of information.

CONTINUOUS SIMPLIFICATION

Companies that begin by publishing an annual calendar with a clear cadence for activities and programs and a predictable system for communication will find that they have made a noticeable and meaningful difference in how simple it is to do business with them.

Once these three tools are implemented, you can begin to identify other opportunities for simplification. For example:

- "How simple is your compensation plan?"
- "How simple is your product story?"
- "How simple is your website?"
- "How simple is your customer acquisition system?"

We never truly arrive at simple. As your company grows and adds people, products and new markets, the fight to keep things simple becomes more and more complex. However, during a turnaround, simplification can help focus resources to improve execution and eliminate programs and people that are a drain on cash.

ADVICE FOR FIELD LEADERS

Simplification for Field Leaders

As is the case for many of the elements of our C.H.I.S.E.L. turnaround formula, the simplification process can be unsettling to a field that does not understand what is happening. While improved communication, an annual calendar and a predictable cadence can help field leaders and will be warmly welcomed, other decisions made to simplify things (reducing the number of products, having fewer promotions or new products, etc.) could be troubling. The first role field leaders can play is to effectively lead their team and reassure them that the company is making the best decisions.

Field leaders can lead simplification efforts for their team by aligning with the company's calendar, cadence and communication... if it has one. Here are a few specific do's and don'ts:

- *DON'T create your own programs if the company already has something.* I'm always surprised when leaders add their own team promotions and incentives on top of company programs. On occasion these can be helpful, but for the most part they are a waste of the leader's time and money and create complexity for everyone involved.
- *DO create a communication system for your team...* and modify it as necessary to make sure it doesn't overlap with the company's communication. This can be particularly helpful if your company hasn't yet simplified communication. If you (with the help of other leaders on your team) can summarize communication and make it easy for your team, do it. Also, follow the counsel given to companies above by having a system for your team that includes a way to communicate with leaders, new sellers, the entire team, and those who are part of "push groups" to achieve specific volume or advancement goals.
- *DO be vocal about supporting company decisions to simplify.* As a leader, it is not enough to passively be "OK" with something. During times of doubt and uncertainty good leaders don't remain silent and allow the negative voices to have the floor. Take the proverbial microphone and make sure your team hears about the good and has information to overcome the naysayers that will surely try and grab attention during these times of change.

CHAPTER 12: EXPANDING TO NEW MARKETS—

Finding New Customers in New Places

"The more that you learn, the more places you'll go."

— DR. SEUSS

N

When most executives think about expansion, they think of *international* expansion. But in the next two chapters I want to broaden your thinking beyond international expansion and encourage you to consider the many domestic expansion opportunities. Most companies have the opportunity to find new markets for their products in their own country. New domestic markets could include new geographies (cities or states), new demographics (retirees or generation Z) and new languages (e.g. U.S. Chinese speakers). The goal is to find new customers in new places that create new opportunities for your field to pursue.

The idealist in me would like to encourage all companies to first perfect their systems (especially their customer acquisition system) in their current market before expanding to new ones. However, I cannot ignore the fact that historically many of the largest direct selling companies used expansion—most often international expansion— to grow themselves out of a downturn and find Renewal. I know of only a few companies that perfected their systems as their primary method of growing. Despite the fact that most renewal has come from international expansion does not mean that there are not good examples of companies who have found growth domestically, there are examples of companies who found growth without needing to acquire a passport and travel to distant countries. Let's start by examining the opportunities for growth in your own domestic "backyard."

CHAPTER 13: EXPANDING TO NEW DOMESTIC MARKETS—
No Passports Required

"Don't believe you have to travel far and wide to discover opportunities. The best opportunities will always be found in your own backyard, and not half way around the world in someone else's backyard. You have to look for them, however."

— ERNIE J. ZELINSKI, AUTHOR

N

When we think of international expansion, we think of Amway, Nu Skin, Jeunesse Global, Avon and other household names. When we think of domestic expansion some of the best examples of Renewal from new U.S. markets include:

- *Melaleuca*—As Melaleuca grew from $20 million to $100 million and then to $200 million, the company did so by tapping into pockets of growth in Minnesota, Orlando and eventually New England. Each of these geographic pockets was essentially a new market and each grew when the company found and supported a new field leader.
- *Princess House*—One of the waves of growth experienced by Princess House included growth in the U.S. Hispanic market for the first time.
- *Herbalife*—Technically they developed the model for their U.S. Hispanic growth in Mexico, but Herbalife saw renewed growth when they introduced Nutrition Clubs to the U.S. Hispanic market.
- *Jafra*—Again, the success of the U.S. market was no doubt aided by their foreign Spanish speaking countries, but Jafra's

U.S. business saw renewed growth when they effectively grew within the U.S. Hispanic market.
- *Amway*—Amway tapped into an entirely new demographic when it first partnered with Energy Drink manufacturer XS (founded by a former Amway distributor) in 2003 and later purchased XS in 2015. In their press release announcing the acquisition, Amway's Chairman Steve Van Andel said, "According to our research, no demographic is more positive about entrepreneurship than those younger than 35, which is the precise target group for the XS brand."[18]

Whether your goal is to discover geographic areas where you have yet to find customers, to expand your reach to a new age segment or to offer your products to customers in the U.S. who prefer to do business in a language other than English, the goal is to identify and develop a strategy to reach customers you're currently not serving.

DOMESTIC GEOGRAPHIC EXPANSION

A few years ago, I participated in a company's strategic planning process as a partner to one of the world's leading strategy consulting firms. We were asked to prepare a five-year strategic plan for a large U.S.-based direct selling company. As you would expect, the consulting firm went through an extensive evaluation and data analysis before they came back with five strategic recommendations. According to their report, the recommendation with the best return on investment was a campaign to focus on white space opportunities in the United States… this despite the fact that the company had yet to start any international expansion. In other words, they showed how the company had grown in a few key states in the South and Midwest and showed that capturing a similar "fair share" of category sales in other states would more than double sales.

From a theoretical perspective, attacking U.S. white space sounds simple, but from a practical standpoint, I have yet to find a direct

[18] https://www.amwayglobal.com/amway-acquires-xs-energy-brand/ accessed on Sept 30, 2019.

selling company that has proven an ability to target geographic expansion within the United States. Don't get me wrong, there are several companies that have had some success. However, our success at Melaleuca, for instance, wasn't due to a specific geographic growth plan we put in place but rather the good fortune of others recruiting strong leaders who grew their business in those new geographies. Geographic targeting, like deciding to grow California, for example, is a strategy waiting for a success story.

It is possible that direct selling companies have not been willing to invest capital in traditional media and that a decision to do so could be key to expanding geographically in the U.S. I hope the channel can figure out how to crack this code as I believe it has so much to offer to urban America and to lower-income neighborhoods. However, if you're going to invest in a geographic expansion plan in the U.S. as your ticket to restart growth, know that you are laying track in a yet untapped wilderness of opportunity.

LANGUAGE EXPANSION OPPORTUNITIES

If the new market you are planning to attack is language-based (e.g. Korean, Spanish), there are more examples of success, but the results are still a mixed success rate. I have seen enough winners to know that there are opportunities to find growth or in some cases to entirely transfer growth to a customer base speaking a new language, but there are also plenty of examples of companies still trying to crack that nut. Here are a few lessons learned that might help you as you consider expanding to new language markets:

- ***U.S. Hispanic as a primer to other Spanish-speaking markets isn't a proven strategy.*** Some companies follow a strategy I pursued: to grow the U.S. Hispanic market as a precursor to opening Mexico and other Spanish-speaking international markets. I have learned the hard way that there are more examples of foreign Spanish-language markets contributing to the growth of the U.S. Hispanic than vice versa. Often U.S. Hispanic citizens no longer have influential contacts in foreign markets and often the Spanish language isn't enough of a common interest to lead to strong networking—for example, few Puerto Rican Spanish speakers have strong networks outside of the Puerto Rican community.

- *Chinese speakers want to know you have a China Strategy.*
There are several examples of how tapping into domestic Chinese speakers opened doors into other Chinese-speaking communities around the world. I've been taught by those with massive success in these markets that it's hard to recruit Chinese-speaking leaders if you can't effectively articulate your plan to sell in China—even if this is many years away.

- *Asian language-speaking communities are great precursors to Asian market expansion.* Nu Skin and Neways (now Modere) are both good examples of how building a strong distributor base within a domestic Asian community can lead to significant sales in foreign markets. Both had huge success in Japan as a result of cultivating strong Japanese-speaking distributors in the U.S. Other companies have had similar success with South Korea. If you are contemplating expansion to a foreign market—especially Asian markets—try growing distributors in the U.S. who speak the language and come from the market you wish to open.

ADVICE FOR FIELD LEADERS

A Domestic Expansion Plan for Field Leaders

Even if your company has not yet announced plans to expand to an international market, you can begin to create and implement your own international expansion plan. The plan could be simple and could contribute to the growth of your business in your current market. For example, you could:

(1) Nurture minorities of all types—Make sure your team is a welcome place for all and that you recognize how difficult it can be to be the "first" to join an organization. When you have your "first" Australian or first Chinese person join your team, reach out to them, ask them how you can help them and do all you can to support their efforts—especially if they are recruiting others and request your help.

(2) Be purposeful—"I'm looking to expand my business to X"— Ask for referrals and let people know you are looking for team members who speak French or have lived in New Zealand.

(3) Follow your warm market—Referrals from your warm market will end up being the strongest team members for you and will in the end be the best way for you to expand to new markets. Ask for referrals and expect that your business will grow through your network and not through cold acquaintances.

(4) Make a list (launch your business from scratch)—So many field leaders were taught to start their business by creating a list of people they know. This simple exercise eludes them when they decide to start building their international business. When you begin your business, start from scratch and create a list of people who have lived or done business in a country and another list of those with language capability. Then start working that list and expanding it via referrals from those on the list.

When business has slowed and you can't figure out how to generate new sales from your current customers/distributors, it is time to begin to look for and plan for opportunities to expand. Whether your plans call for expansion into new states or new language markets, finding new customers and creating new opportunities for your distributors to grow their business is a tried and true method of Renewal.

RENEWAL

CHAPTER 14: EXPANDING TO INTERNATIONAL MARKETS—
Finding the Majority of Today's Sales

"You will either step forward into growth or you will step back into safety."

— **ABRAHAM MASLOW, PSYCHOLOGIST**

In 2018 (the most recent data reported) global direct sales totaled $193 billion with approximately 18% ($35.4 billion) coming from the U.S. Many of the largest direct selling companies mimic these global statistics and report more than 80% of their sales outside the U.S. Given these statistics, the opportunity for geographic expansion is real, but it is also true that most companies with international operations have multiple countries losing money.

Perhaps because so many companies have international markets that lose money, I've met some CEOs who have been hesitant to expand internationally. These executives typically argue that they have barely tapped their U.S. market potential. "Why would I want to spend my limited time and resources elsewhere?" they argue.

It is true that most direct sellers have plenty of upside opportunity in the U.S., but it is crucial for executives to understand one fact: NO direct selling company has reached and sustained a billion dollars in sales in the United States alone (some have more than a billion now, but I don't know of any that didn't expand beyond the U.S. first.) Even some of the largest companies have found it difficult to sustain $500 million in U.S. sales over a long period of time. If you choose to bet on a U.S.-only strategy, realize that you risk losing momentum if your company is growing with sales north of $600 million.

During my tenure at USANA, we had one of the channel's most successful international executives, Bradford Richardson, leading our international expansion efforts. Under his leadership, I played only a supporting role in international expansion, but I had a chance to learn from his success. Bradford led the international business for both USANA Health Sciences and later Shaklee. At both of these companies, he showed how valuable international expansion can be to a direct selling company.

While at USANA we were able to use pricing to renew the distributors' belief in the company, but had we not started on the path of global expansion about the same time, we would have not experienced the long-term growth the company has had over the past two decades. International expansion is a key component to long-term growth in direct selling and often companies err in being too aggressive or too slow to pursue it. I've seen companies wait too long before they expand to new markets and they miss out on the benefit of momentum. Expanding during a company's momentum years is beneficial for both the company and for distributors who have greater cash flow available during those periods to personally invest in building their business in new international markets. Likewise, some companies make the decision to open several (sometimes a dozen or more) new markets in as many months and find themselves with lots of new costs and little new business.

Successful International Launch Tactics

I learned many valuable tips from watching Richardson and from studying the successful expansion of other companies like Nu Skin. For example, *make sure you have field leaders with contacts and who have a willingness to go* and build their business in the market(s) you intend to open. I believe it is better to start with a smaller market where you have leaders ready to help you than to focus on a large opportunity without field support. While data showing the popularity of your product category in a country is directional and helpful, it pales in comparison to your leaders' relationships and/or willingness to build in a market.

Unlike a traditional retail business, direct selling companies don't attack geographies with a map and a checkbook. They are not able to identify white space in a specific state or region and decide that they will invest in building a few new stores there next. Direct selling companies don't have the ability to tell the field what to do or where to sell. They only have influence on their field. Looking at geographical white space, whether in the U.S. or internationally, might be a sign of opportunity, but it isn't as formulaic as it would be if working with a brick-and-mortar retailer.

Direct sellers exploit white space opportunity only if they are able to find volunteers from within the current distributor base with relationships in the areas they hope to grow. In other words, too often companies open a new market expecting to have sales success without having leaders who are interested in building in that new market. The great international success stories most often include local success among current distributors with contacts in the targeted markets. For example, in one of my interviews I learned of a company that had only opened one market—the Philippines. They were having amazing success; in fact, that market was growing to be larger than their U.S. market.

"Why did you choose to go to the Philippines of all places?" I asked.

"Because we had strong leaders and solid success among Filipinos in the U.S., and they took us there," was the answer.

Executives like to believe they are in charge and can direct the geographic expansion of a direct selling company. However, the most successful companies are those working with their current field leaders and developing diverse distributors in their current markets, and then allowing their leaders to lead them to new geographies.

More than one executive has expressed frustration with their field's lack of interest in international development. While a few companies have successfully expanded into new international markets without the support of the field in their initial market, the most effective and efficient way to grow into new markets is to do so with the leaders in your current market forging the way. Therefore, I would make sure there is ample evidence that the company's current leaders want to expand their business and/or have the language and/or skills to build an international business.

In my experience, if you don't have leaders who will go to new markets or who have relationships in those markets, then your probability of success is pretty low. Companies that have success internationally are those that first do a great job developing leaders in their current markets. A good example is Nu Skin, which had tremendous success in Japan in the 80s and 90s... but that success came as a result of first growing among Japanese Americans, primarily in Hawaii.

I asked one of the channel's top consultants, Paul Adams, about the key to international expansion.

"I'm a total believer that the leadership needs to take you there, not you take the leaders there," he replied.

If that statement is true—and I believe it is—you'd better have leaders ready and willing to expand internationally, or a plan to develop leaders who will support your strategy.

When we reference "leader-led" international expansion, it is essential to note that we are not saying that a company should open any market in which their top leaders claim to have contacts. Too many companies have destroyed their profitability and reputation chasing leader's international expansion whims. My definition of leader-led global expansion includes a thoughtful business analysis of where to go that includes a substantial weighting of those markets where current leaders have language skills, contacts or are reasonably confident in their ability to find connections, and a willingness to travel and work in the market.

Another valuable tip I've learned over the years is to ***invest in hiring experienced management*** with international experience and especially with experience in a particular country or region you plan to open.

When our children were younger my wife and I decided to take them to visit Machu Picchu and the jungles of Peru. My brother traveled with us. Looking back on that trip, I probably would have not taken such young kids had I known what I know now. Every day was an adventure not to be forgotten, but on one particular day we hiked about a mile through the jungle to a freshwater lake for a little fishing and swimming. Our experienced guides cut our way through a spider web 15 feet wide by 6 feet high that was filled with spiders. Eventually we came to the edge of a large, beautiful lake with towering trees growing from the water and a long wood canoe tied to one of the trees. Our guides helped us board the canoe and paddle our way to the far corner of the lake. One guide took fresh meat from his knapsack and tied it to a hook on the end of a stick; this was our fishing pole. He invited two of my young children to stand in the canoe and throw the line in the water and told us we would be catching piranha. The fact that our three-year-old was casting for flesh eating fish wasn't enough to worry us, but after more than 20 minutes with no bites we couldn't help but notice that our guides looked increasingly alarmed.

Suddenly I saw something out of the corner of my eye that I thought was imaginary. I'd never seen anything like it and couldn't figure out what it was. At first, I thought maybe it was just a large tree root but then realized it was moving. I saw a huge hump that looked to be about twelve inches or more in diameter come out of the water. It kind of looked like a mythical monster though I couldn't see a head or a tail.

"Did anyone else see that?" I asked.

"I did," my wife replied, her eyes wide.

No one else seemed to pay attention so my wife and I talked to each other about this strange sight for a minute. Suddenly one of the guides stopped what he was doing and asked, "What did you say? What did you see?"

When we described what we had seen he leaped to the center of the canoe, grabbed my daughter and pulled in her line. He said something in Spanish to the other guide and they immediately began to row us to the center of the lake. My brother, who speaks Spanish, asked him why he had done that and he replied, "Anaconda!" He said that they never fail to catch piranha at that spot and the one thing that would scare away piranha is an anaconda. He told us that these snakes are the only animals that can see out of the water, and they are known for attacking humans and pulling them from boats. He, in fact, had been pulled from a boat and saved by a friend with a machete who cut him free from the massive snake. To prove his point, he raised his shirt and showed us the scars on his body. My wife and I had indeed seen the mid-section of a very large anaconda—a sight we had never seen before and hope to never see again. Our guides were moving us to deeper water where the snakes wouldn't swim.

What would have happened if we had tried to go fishing for piranha without an experienced guide? Would my daughter have become a victim that day or would we have just ended our expedition empty handed? It's impossible to know, but I can tell you that we were very grateful to have an expert guide with us that day. I won't choose to explore any foreign wilderness without one, you can be sure of that! While international markets can be exciting and very lucrative if done right, too often companies choose to figure out new markets on their own without the help of an experienced guide. Oftentimes companies choose individuals by virtue of the language they speak, or a previous tourist with just a small amount of experience in a foreign market. Like my wife and I, they don't even know what dangers to look for because they don't have the familiarity it takes to recognize when something is not quite right.

The industry is littered with tales of companies that lost millions due to the fact that they lacked international expertise. There are stories of companies with local managers imprisoned because the organization failed to fully comply with local laws. More than one company has paid out more than 100% of their product revenue because they failed to understand local return laws and had never had their compensation plan fully tested. When distributors in the new market "maximized their plan" and took advantage of generous return laws, the initial euphoria from their "amazing launch" turned to ruin and dejection overnight.

Not long ago I interviewed a rising star, an executive who had just been tasked with leading international expansion for a large company. This young executive had never led international expansion, but after talking with several other executives and counseling with his team, he was ready to attack Asia because "that's where all our competitors are growing." He then told me that the first country he was recommending would be Japan, and he believed the company could be open for business in six months. When asked why Japan, he said that two of his team members had done business there. They knew the language and were convinced the venture would be a success.

I followed up that discussion with a confidential conversation with a CFO who had just helped a competitor launch in Japan and learned that it had taken her more than a year just to secure a banking relationship. Others confirmed that the regulatory challenges would take longer than six months and still others warned that it had been several years since a U.S. company had succeeded in Japan. None had done so without first having strong Japanese contacts. This particular firm had none.

I tell this story to remind executives that it takes more than great management skills, a proven track record of U.S. sales leadership or even language or foreign experience. Growing a solid international business is more likely to happen and serious mistakes are more likely to be avoided if you have someone with previous experience leading the effort... or at least hire consultants who understand the regulatory and financial nuances of foreign markets.

My final tip for a successful international launch is *don't rush it*. Make sure the company has a plan with plenty of time built in for required product registration and licensing (this can take months or more than a year depending on the market). How fast can you enter a new market? According to former CFO and current author and speaker Devin Thorpe, "About a year or ten months if you push it."

"If you have an extremely competent international expansion, then it varies probably by market, but it takes about a year," Devin continued. "Regulatory approval takes time. It doesn't matter how many engineers you put on it, the regulatory approvals take time. And if you push it, you run the risk of testing the Foreign Corrupt Practices Act."

While most companies go into international markets with the proper product or opportunity registrations, a few have decided to sidestep local laws. Most international markets have product registration laws, and a few (like Canada) have business opportunity or compensation plan regulations.

I conducted an interview with the president of a mid-market international direct selling company who asked not to be identified.

"There are so many companies that expand to international markets using an NFR [not for resale] model," he explained. "They have a tremendous amount of business internationally, but they're not well established in any market. They don't know if their compensation plan is legal. They don't have the licensing set up. They don't have their product registered, and if it's not done right, sales can dry up pretty fast. And I've seen it happen."

Take your time and make sure you are going into a country through the front door with all of the regulatory approvals you need to sell via your compensation system and to market your company's products.

Choosing International Markets

Where should you go if you're thinking about international expansion? The short answer is "wherever your leaders have the best contacts and a willingness to travel and build." The data would say that while there are a few (mostly local) direct sellers who have had success in Europe or South America, most international success still comes from Asia. If you don't have leaders with a desire to expand and grow their business internationally, often you can find these leaders in Canada or Australia. Both of these countries have traditionally been places where you can enroll distributors with more international experience and contacts, and though small in number, they can be strategically important. Mexico, though large, has been a mixed market for many and the United Kingdom has been both a disaster and a bonanza depending on the company and the in-country management.

In choosing international markets, you're looking for evidence that there is demand for your product, confirmation that you can clear the country's product and direct selling regulatory hurdles, assurance that you can access dollars earned in the market and you want to make sure that the economics will make the business profitable. All of those variables are important, but the one veto variable is having leaders who can and will build in that new market.

China is one of the most dynamic markets for direct sellers and should be a cornerstone of any company's international expansion plans. Bradford Richardson, the former president of Shaklee International and one of the channel's most successful international executives, believes that having at least a blueprint for China is key. "Even if you don't plan on going to China immediately, you have to have a China strategy before you launch operations in any other country," he said. "Sooner or later your international leaders will be asking you about your China strategy."

China has been a very successful market for the large direct sellers who entered the market early. Unfortunately, the government has slowed almost to a stop the issuing of new direct selling licenses, making the country a significant challenge to companies not doing business there now. Some companies have found it critical to have Chinese partners to help them navigate the politics and cultural nuances there. In the past two decades, a few have made acquisitions or entered into mergers to assist them in their China business.

For example, in 2010 USANA Health Sciences, Inc. (NASDAQ: USNA) acquired BabyCare Ltd, a China-based direct selling company. In the press release announcing the deal, Dave Wentz, then USANA's chief executive officer, said, "We are very excited about this acquisition and the opportunity that it provides for USANA to ultimately establish a business via BabyCare in China... As a company with over eleven years of in-country experience, and as one of <u>only twenty-five companies operating with a direct selling license in China</u>, BabyCare brings us both valuable knowledge of China's direct selling market and the ability to expand our business in China via BabyCare. We believe this acquisition is the most effective way for us to enter this enormous market."

Four years later, Nature's Sunshine Products, Inc. (NASDAQ: NATR) created a joint venture with Shanghai Fosun Pharmaceutical (Group) Co., Ltd. to market and distribute Nature's Sunshine and Synergy products in China.

ADVICE FOR FIELD LEADERS

International Expansion for Field Leaders

As I wrote earlier in this chapter, field leaders are a key ingredient to the success of any expansion and especially when opening new markets. Field leaders should recognize these new international markets as opportunities to grow their business several times its current size and therefore should consider these new markets as a business investment. Leaders who invest their time and money in new markets are more likely to reap the benefits of these markets. Here are some of the tactics successful international field leaders employ to make the most of expansion:

- *Invest Your Time in New Markets*—Today so much can be done via conference call, video conferencing and social media, but the most successful international leaders invest dedicated and meaningful time in each new market. Prospects and up-and-coming leaders need to have in-person time and enough of it to make sure they can become self-sufficient.
- *Systems for Building In-Market Leadership*—Sometimes leaders can "do it all" for their team in the United States, but time zones, language and distance combine to make it impossible for them to effectively nurture and grow a team in a foreign country. Only those who have a commitment to and system for developing local leaders will see their team grow and develop in a new foreign market.
- *Cultural Education*—Taking time to learn as much as possible about the country and its culture will go a long way in gaining the trust and loyalty of a team in a foreign country.
- *Sponsoring High in the Social Status*—Leaders who are able to attract respected citizens of a foreign country are likely to have more success than starting out by sponsoring the working class. In many countries (especially in Asia), class matters more than in the U.S., and recruiting up is so much more difficult than starting with professionals and expanding from there. Take the time to network with and begin your efforts high in the country's ranks of social status.
- *Growing in Your Market First*—As soon as your company announces a new market, I would immediately begin to try and find those with in-country and/or language experience. For example, if you are going to Japan, start by finding Japanese speakers and Japanese living in the U.S.
- *Support the Company Even if You Don't Go*—Even if your current

situation doesn't allow you to grow your team in a new market, the company's success in that market can benefit you directly when someone on your team recruits someone from that country, or indirectly by making your company more financially stable or making your opportunity more attractive to other potential distributors.

CHAPTER 15: LEADING DURING TOUGH TIMES—
Being Present and Positive

> "A good leader doesn't get stuck behind a desk."
>
> — **RICHARD BRANSON**

N

George Washington is without peer in human history. He was the first to lead a colonial army to victory, the first to become the undisputed leader of the newly conquered country and then, at his own insistence, to voluntarily limit his term of office and step aside so that there would be a second president of the United States of America. Those who met Washington in his years as General of the Continental Army said that there was never a man more fitted for his role in history than he.

When Washington took command of the ragtag group of volunteer militia that he would later label the "Continental Army," he was humbled by the trust the Continental Congress had put in him and eager to prove worthy of that trust. However, he had no idea how ill-prepared his men were to fight. It took them eight days to produce a simple count of the men under his command. His army had no uniforms, few reliable guns, and a woefully small amount of gunpowder available.

Washington and his army camped for months with nothing to show for their efforts. They were at a standstill with the British and neither side was willing to risk an offensive. Despite Washington's urging, the Generals that made up his "Counsel on War" refused to support him when on four separate occasions he petitioned them with a proposal to attack the British.

In December 1775, the contracts of most of his army expired and thousands returned to their homes rather than wait out a New England winter as soldiers for a stalled army. During this time, Washington, the man who would go down in history as of one of the finest leaders in the world, lamented in a private letter to a friend:

> *The reflection upon my situation and that of this army produces many an uneasy hour, when all around me are wrapped in sleep. Few people know the predicament that we are in. There is too little powder. Still no money.*

Washington, like many a leader before and after him, was discouraged and took this moment in history—months before the Declaration of Independence would be penned and signed—to feel sorry for himself and to wish he had never taken on the role of leader. He wrote:

> *I have often thought how much happier I should have been if instead of accepting of a command under such circumstances, I had taken my musket upon my shoulders and entered the ranks, or if I could have justified the measure to posterity, and my own conscience, and I had retired to the back country and lived in a wigwam. If I shall be able to rise superior to these and many other difficulties which might be enumerated, I shall most religiously believe that the finger of Providence is upon us.*

Leadership—especially in difficult times—is not easy and many a leader like the great George Washington has no doubt wished that they could hide or that they never would have become a leader in the first place. It is in these times that one must be conscious of the natural tendency we have to shrink and wish to lead from a safe place. Too often, when companies are struggling, I have counseled with leaders who have stopped doing all of the things that led to success in the past. They reduced or eliminated field meetings, stopped traveling (citing a lack of funds to pay for travel expenses) and opted to use email and other forms of written communication to fulfill their responsibilities.

It is during these times, when everything in us wants to be behind a desk, that we most need to be with and lead our employees, executive teams, and field sales force. It is OK not to have the answer to your current problems, but it is not OK to hope that the answer will come to you as if by magic. You must strike out and find the answers to the question "How will we renew growth?" Even during times when you can't articulate the path forward, you can articulate your vision of what is possible and have confidence that if you speak your vision often enough, some listener will believe sufficiently to blaze the way forward.

If you are the founder of a company, the CEO, or head of sales, or if you've been charged with leading sales in a region of the world for your company, then you need to be ever present in times of decline. You need to continue to:

- *Find and recognize those who are having success!*
- *Tell your story*—Both the story of your founding and the story of your future and your vision for what your company can be to the world.
- *Be listening and learning*—In person to those who are having challenges and especially to those who are having success.
- *Be Honest*—About where you are and about your determination to work with your team to find your way back to growth.
- *Be Hopeful*—You need to muster the inner strength and find reasons to have hope. Hope cannot be faked. It won't work unless you actually are filled with hope.

ADVICE FOR FIELD LEADERS
Field Leader's & Founder/CEO's Leadership Role

Whether you are a corporate leader or a field leader there are activities you should begin during good times and continue during tough times to make sure you are able to lead your team to Renewal and growth. These activities include:

- *Make Your Team Sticky*—Great leaders make others feel like they are part of something and that they are committed to something bigger than themselves. They make it hard for others to leave by making sure others feel that there are people on the team who care personally about their success.
- *Communicate Through Challenges*—Tough times bring opportunities for tough talks or the risk of strained relationships. Milan Jensen, founder of Womenkind, is one of the world's great connectors. She has worked magic with field leaders who seemed to dislike one another so much that others had given up on them. Milan described for me a session she once led with the leaders of a small company. All the field leaders, including the founder, were convinced that one of the top leaders was on her way out. They were so concerned about her loyalty that they actually considered not inviting her to this retreat of less than ten of the company's top leaders at the top leadership rank.

  Milan told me about a day of sharing that seemed to come to a head when the leader in question challenged the others, and rather than fight, the others listened. They asked her to help them understand why she felt the way she did. By the end of the day, the leader who was assuredly "on her way out" tearfully reassured the others and said, "I never wanted to leave." She just wanted to be heard. During tough times, learning to both listen and share are essential skills for effective leaders.

- *Be Free with Your Grace*—While I am offering you a formula with variables that should be part of your turnaround efforts, I'm not offering a guaranteed plan and I have had both amazing success and very public failures in my efforts to lead turnarounds. Turnarounds are tough and assuredly there will be mistakes made along the way. Field leaders need to expect and allow for failed company programs and resist the urge to blame the management team for the decline.

  Likewise, corporate leaders need to understand that most periods of Hyper-Growth promote unprepared individuals into leadership positions they are not fully equipped to execute flawlessly. Both company and field leaders need to be offered grace, time and resources to help them figure out the business challenges they are suddenly forced to solve during the Shake-Out stage.

- *Be Present*—Your team needs to see you, hear from you and be in rooms with you—now more than ever. As much as your insecurity about your new reality may leave you wanting to be alone, it is during these tough times that your teams need you... live. As tight as cash can be, you must make other cuts to allow you to maintain money to invest in being present.

  Should you risk being in public if you don't have any answers? YES! Showing up just to assure your team that you're on the job "figuring things out" is so much more valuable to your company than your absence and the fertile ground that creates for your team's greatest fears to flourish like yet-to-be-pulled weeds.

- *Invest in Yourself and Your Team*—If you ask network marketing expert Eric Worre, he will tell you that often Hyper-Growth stalls and decline follows because a company grew faster than its ability to grow its leadership. With too few leaders, sales must correct itself by declining to match the level of leadership. If this is the case, then those in leadership—both in the field and in the company—owe it to their teams to invest in their personal development and to learn as much and as fast as they can to improve their ability to lead. Great leaders will read books, listen to lectures and hire experienced advisors to help them accelerate their growth and fill in for the blindness their inexperience often brings.

A RATIONAL LOOK AT "IRRATIONAL" FIELD FEARS

I want to end this chapter with one of the most important lessons of my career and one that forever changed my relationship with those with whom I have worked in the field. During times of sales decline, it is easy for corporate leaders to be surprised by feelings of intense mistrust and anger from field leaders who have previously been so positive. I experienced this early in my career when one of the leaders I respected the most began to show and express deep mistrust and doubt about most of the proposals the corporate team proposed. My initial reaction was to label her "ungrateful," but I knew inside that was not true. One afternoon I drove to meet with her and her husband in their home and in that environment, with no verbal instruction, I learned the following lesson...

For those of us with a corporate salary, it is fairly easy to make a career change and expect to replace and perhaps even improve our income. It is not that simple for field leaders. Those who have built a large sales team and earned a sizeable income from scratch don't have the opportunity to take that team to another company and replace that income elsewhere (I realize some companies promise that to leaders but in reality, it rarely happens). The idea of rebuilding another sales team seems impossible—or at the very least, not desirable.

These top leaders begin to realize how dependent they are on the company they represent and the management of that company. They realize that their earnings can be significantly impacted by things completely out of their control. Given this anxiety, many top leaders become more risk averse for fear that any changes made by the company could significantly impact their income and lifestyle. This trepidation often is interpreted by management as being "negative" or "emotional" rather than "grateful" and "logical."

Corporate leaders should recognize how vulnerable their field leaders are and should openly acknowledge their desire to help the leaders persevere and then grow the business they have built. Likewise, field leaders should recognize the psychology of their position and avoid allowing their fears to go unchecked and express themselves in aggressive and negative behavior to corporate leadership... and especially to impact the hope and confidence of their team.

RENEWAL

CHAPTER 16: BEYOND YOUR C.H.I.S.E.L.—

Other Considerations That Impact Pace

"Perspective is worth 80 IQ points."

— ALAN KAY, SCIENTIST

While the variables we have introduced make up the core ingredients of a successful turnaround, employing them effectively requires context and perspective of the company and the organization. I have learned through sad experience that organizations, precisely because of the humans that compose them, need much attention and attentiveness to their attitude and disposition in order to reach their full potential.

CHANGE FATIGUE

For Christmas in 2016 my wife convinced me to surprise our youngest daughter with a dog that she had "earned" and I had tried in vain to avoid. The video of her uncontrollable joy and tender tear-filled reception of a little four-pound Morkie (Maltese/Yorkie mix) by the name of Jack went viral over the next few days,[19] and in spite of my reluctance, I became a bit of a folk hero for my part in acquiring this new pet. That would not be the end of my role because Jack decided that I would be his Alpha. On most days he follows me around begging me to take him for a walk or give him a treat. Even with his zealous begging for a walk, I have found on several occasions that Jack's enthusiasm for walking often ends before my intended route is complete. Jack has learned to abandon his spot in front leading me along the path and instead take up a position between my feet, making

[19] https://youtu.be/BlKpTKO4UHo

it almost impossible for me to walk. When I look down, he looks up and I've now been trained to pick him up and carry him the rest of the way home.

Our organizations can be a lot like Jack. Even though they are excited and aware of the need to hurry through the trail of tough times, the team's stamina doesn't always keep pace with that of their leaders. A wise leader will recognize when it is necessary to put things on pause, slow the pace, or find a way to give team members a rest.

This is particularly an issue when a new CEO joins a company that has already been through significant change and turmoil. The new leader arrives full of new ideas and new programs and is "fresh" because s/he hasn't been through the same exhausting challenges the legacy staff and sellers have. I've made the mistake of failing to show proper respect for the amount of change an organization has been through and suffered through poor execution and lackluster results when trying to push my own agenda on a worn-out staff or field sales force.

A wise leader recognizes that change fatigue is real and that sometimes the pace for the way forward needs to be recalibrated. This is a good perspective for leaders of turnarounds to have.

MANAGEMENT TEAM

We have talked about changing multiple aspects of a company but have not mentioned the fact that sometimes due to skill, performance, or mindset, members of a company's management team must change. I have made the mistake of being slow to remove good people I really liked despite the fact that I knew they were not fully in support of making the changes necessary for the company to achieve Renewal. In almost every case my hesitance came at a cost to me, the organization... and, ironically, the person I was trying to be kind to.

In his book *Thinking, Fast and Slow*, Daniel Kahneman writes that each one of us keeps a mental scorecard of our successes and failures. He argues that too often we fail not because our ideas don't work, but because we don't admit that they don't work and we fail to pivot to new ones. Kahneman claims that many executives who have recently failed are reluctant to take necessary risks for fear of being wrong again. These executives are not helpful to a company—especially one in need of experimentation as part of a turnaround effort. He writes:

> *Boards of directors are well aware of these conflicts and often replace a CEO who is encumbered by prior decisions and reluctant to cut losses. The members of the board do not necessarily believe that the new CEO is more competent than the one she replaces. They do know that she does not carry the same mental accounts and is therefore better able to ignore the sunk costs of past investments in evaluating current opportunities.*

As you lead turnaround efforts in your company, be keenly aware of the capabilities and biases of your current management team and quickly assess if they are up for the transformational work ahead. If not, and if a break isn't enough to get them on board, making a change sooner than later is in everyone's best interest.

REINVESTING IN YOUR COMPANY

Several years ago, I received a phone call from a friend who started a direct selling company and in partnership with a private equity firm had leveraged the company with significant debt. When sales performance began to fall well short of previous results and well below the projections given the lender, the lender launched a series of meetings during which they demanded that the founder reinvest several million dollars. This lender wanted the founder to take money that had been distributed previously and invest it back into the business (primarily in the form of retiring some of the outstanding debt). The founder asked for my opinion on whether I thought their family should put the money back in the business.

Knowing nothing about the personal finances of this founder and not being qualified to advise the family on the wisdom of this investment in comparison to other investments they might choose, the best I could do was encourage the founder to make an appeal to values. I asked if they had hope or belief that the company would rebound and if they still cared about the business and felt like it was worthy of their time. I then posed a question I love to ask whenever someone is having difficulty making a tough and weighty decision: "What would bring you more regret, the thought of the business failing or the thought of losing this money in an effort to save it?"

This founder chose—against the advice of financial and legal advisors—to reinvest in the business. To date they have lost all the money and the operation shows little hope of producing enough revenue to ever repay it. She has, however, been able to keep the business open and has helped tens of thousands of distributors earn and grow for several years, as of this writing.

Many founders will be faced with the decision of whether or not to reinvest in their declining company. My business sense leads me to caution against it. Still, I haven't met a founder yet who, when given the chance, chose NOT to double down on the business they founded. My advice to them is more practical: work closely with your financial and legal advisors to assure your family's wellbeing and limit your reinvestment to money that will not put them at risk for hardship in the future. Reinvest with the expectation that you will not see the money again and then work to get it back with all the determination you would have if that money was essential for your future.

ADVICE FOR FIELD LEADERS

Founder/CEO & Field Leader Self-Care

As you embark on a turnaround, you will need the support of those close to you and you will need to be disciplined about caring for your mental, emotional and physical health. Turnarounds are draining.

Most often they are marathons that require you to run at sprint-like speed. Not only can they take a toll on your physical health, but they can introduce significant stress into the life of your family (spouse and children). They strain all of your relationships as you are forced to spend more time at work, on the road, or even worse, to fire friends and co-workers to whom you have been close.

Hire a coach or a team of coaches to help you through the challenges of your life and business. Don't expect yourself to be an expert in every area of life. Recognize the value of receiving help and support from experts who have been down this road that is so foreign to you now. Take vacation—a minimum of two weeks a year and preferably one week a quarter. Yes, I'm recommending that you take more time for yourself and your family, even during those times when your business seems to need you the most. You might be pleasantly surprised at how quickly the answers to your toughest business challenges come when your mind is in vacation mode rather than nonstop crisis management mode.

GET CREATIVE AT CELEBRATION

The fatigue of always seeing a falling scorecard can be overwhelming to you and your team. Every team wants to win. Finding meaningful and realistic milestones and successes you can celebrate will require creativity and mindfulness. In other words, train yourself and your team to establish milestones you are likely to be able to celebrate and to be on the lookout for things worth celebrating. Then... take the time to celebrate them!

RENEWAL

CHAPTER 17: WHEN YOU FAIL TO RENEW—

Other Options When Growth Doesn't Happen

"Success is not final; failure is not fatal."

— **WINSTON CHURCHILL**

N

Several years ago, I received a call from an investor who had an interest in a direct selling company that at one point had sales of several hundred million dollars. This company had seen sales decline to $150 million and the private equity owner had decided to liquidate it at all cost. This investor had the chance to purchase the company for pennies on the dollar and came to me with the question, "If you were me, would you buy this company?"

I met with the current management team, reviewed the financials, product offering and history, and a few weeks later called the investor to report that I would not make the purchase. He was surprised but patient, and followed my advice. A few days later the company was sold for less than $20 million to another direct seller who would make the products available but who really wanted the field leaders that were still left.

I concluded that this company was beyond Renewal and that it was unlikely it would ever regain growth because of the shaky foundation and lack of discipline the field had experienced. I'm not sure my decision was correct, but it is not the only time in my life I've come to a similar conclusion, and not the only company I've seen in similar straits. In fact, just as I set out to write this book, I had a call with the owner of a company that was producing sales of just 20% of what it had been producing two years earlier. This company also had debt. The founder's question to me was, "How much do you think I could sell the company for?" My answer was a disappointing amount, much less than the debt owed at the time.

The sad reality is that sometimes, businesses fail. Not all of them can be saved. Some, like Herbalife, will survive the Shake-Out stage and others, like Longaberger, will not.[20] We have given you a set of tools and advice to help ensure that your company experiences Renewal rather than failure, but if it does not show signs of revitalization, what are your options? What should you do?

Let me offer the following advice from my personal experience and the experience of others I've studied:

- *Maintain a long-term view*—As Winston Churchill stated, "Failure is not fatal" and even though you may lose the company you are leading now, it doesn't mean your business life is over. Yesterday I had a very exciting phone call with the founder of a company that was off to an impressive start. He had attracted notable investors, a strong board and excellent field leaders to help him launch his second direct selling company after his first was forced to close a few years ago. As you make decisions to stop, save, or sell your current company, do so with a long-term view in mind and with the expectation that the choices you make will have an impact on your future. In other words, whatever you do, act with class… but don't be afraid to close a failing business.
- *Finding a home for the field*—While you may not be able to find a buyer for your company, you should have no problem finding a home for your field. Often, if you will look for a partner who will take good care of your field leaders, you will also find a partner who will provide you some financial benefit for helping them on-board your distributors. Field leaders rarely go en masse from one company

---

[20] Ironically, just as we are preparing to publish this book the Longaberger family is attempting to relaunch the company starting with an appearance on QVC.

to the next. I'm told by one investor group with experience that they typically expect to save just 50% of a company's distributors. Founders and executives who do their best to make decisions that they think are in the best interest of their field will preserve relationships and keep their options alive for years and companies to come.

o *The Field Announcement*—When I was CEO of Jewel Kade, we were acquired by Thirty-One Gifts and I was honestly excited about the opportunities that new relationship would offer our field leaders. However, I realized that our field leaders would be very disappointed by the news and I felt like they deserved to have as much personal interaction as possible. We therefore invited the top-ranking distributors to a live announcement at Thirty-One Gift's headquarters and then held a series of conference calls to make the announcements and answer questions. I went on the road and held dozens of small cottage meetings around the country where distributors of all ranks could come to learn more about why I believed this announcement was good news for the field and to answer their questions. Despite some disappointment—and much emotion—the field leaders respected the fact that as CEO I was accountable and willing to face them in person and to respect their feelings and insight.

o *Where to look for partners*—The best place to look for a home for your field is to start with companies with similar values and ideally with similar products and selling styles. Hopefully you are and will be attending industry events and forming relationships with executives who may eventually be on the other end of the phone. If you can't think of a company or don't have those kinds of relationships, there are a few companies in the industry who have shown an interest in acquiring the field leaders of other companies. They include:

Youngevity
BeneYOU

ARIIX
Vorwerk
Xyngular

- *Finding a home for your employees*—When it became time to announce that Jewel Kade would be acquired by Thirty-One Gifts, it was the middle of December, just weeks away from Christmas. There is never a good time of year to tell your employees that they will no longer have a job, but I can't think of a worse time for employees to receive such news. Fortunately, we had several weeks to prepare for that announcement and the founders at Jewel Kade vowed that they would do all in their power to help their employees find work. Accordingly, we reached out to local companies that we knew were growing and confidentially told them about our impending announcement. Several of them were interested in hiring our employees and the day after our announcement we held an onsite job fair and, with the exception of a few of us senior executives, were able to place all the employees who were ready and wanted to work. You may have no legal requirement to assist your employees on the way out, but doing all you can for them will be remembered by them... and the wider business community. It will also help you feel so much better about what is undoubtedly a very painful decision and process.

ADVICE FOR FIELD LEADERS

Field Leaders – Finding Your "Next"

No matter what a company decides to do, field leaders have their own decision to make if and when their company doesn't make it or perhaps when their income falls below a sustainable level. Those who were earning full-time income may decide to fill in their loss with a part-time or full-time job, or they may decide that it is time to go in a different direction altogether. If you are a field leader looking for a new company, let me offer you some suggestions for what to look for and what to avoid, but first a few words of advice:

- *Speed vs. Resolve*—While you may feel pressure to find something fast, especially if you risk losing your team to another company, don't let speed trump resolve. In other words, don't join a company just because you feel like you don't have time to find something better. Building a direct selling business is difficult, even when you bring the strength of a team that has worked together in the past. But it is excruciatingly painful when you realize you're building a business for a company that doesn't share your values or whose product you don't love. If forced to choose to go fast or to wait for the right thing—wait.
- *Test, then Scale*—Don't be afraid to test a company you think will be great. Try the product, even try selling and sponsoring for a few weeks, but if you discover along the way that the product or company is not all you hoped for, DO NOT SETTLE. It is perfectly OK to switch companies a few days, weeks or even months into a "next company" experience. In the end you will be so, so happy that you had the integrity to find the right fit. Once you've fallen in love with your new company and feel it's a good match, go fast and hard and scale your business.

"I just couldn't do it!"

Recently I received a call from a former employee who was so excited about her first VP role in a company that was growing and well known. She asked a few questions and we ended the conversation with her voice full of energy. Less than two months later, this same friend called back and sheepishly described the short tenure she had at the company she'd been so excited about initially. She said, "Brett, when I learned the truth about the CEO and her values, I just couldn't stay."

Perhaps she thought I would think less of her, but I thought more highly of her than ever before and we went to work together to find a fit she felt great about.

FINDING A NEW HOME—WHAT TO LOOK FOR

When it is time to find a new home, here are the things I would look for if I were joining a company as a field leader:

- *Product Fit*—I don't think anything else matters as much. If you aren't in love with the product and excited about using it every day for the rest of your life, this is not the company for you.
- *Culture/Value Fit*—Often you can't really understand the values and culture of a company in the interview process, but you can ask values-based questions and you can look to see if they are attracting others who share your same values. Even if you find out after you join, run away as fast as you can if you find a company whose values are not in tune with your own.
- *Customer Focus*—In today's regulatory and social environment, if your company is "opportunity focused" and not consumer or product focused, I don't believe you will last. In my opinion, the only sustainable model for direct sellers requires that they focus on selling products to consumers, and then converting delighted customers into distributors.
- *Momentum*—If you are forced to look for a second company, momentum should matter to you. Avoid those who are reaching the peak of Hyper-Growth (three to five years into it) and those in a decline. Instead, look for companies that are just experiencing growth or even better, those who have been through Hyper-Growth and are experiencing Renewal and growth after a period of flattening or decline.
- *Systems*—Your chance of success is much greater if the company or the team you are joining has proven systems for attracting customers, upgrading customers to distributors, on-boarding distributors, helping distributors get to profitability, and developing leaders. Having all those systems in place is the ideal, but at the very least having an excellent customer

acquisition system is essential.

- *Consumable Products*—While your passion might be jewelry or vacuums or cookware, history has proven that your direct selling business is likely to be more successful over time if the products you sell are consumable and lend themselves to frequent reorders. Even better, if your company has a consumer friendly (not comp plan friendly) subscription program, your job as a distributor will be so much easier.

- *Management Team*—Management that shows a commitment to doing the right thing for the right reason is essential. Too many direct selling executives have become celebrities in their own company, and they make decisions that preserve their popularity at the expense of running a great business. If the executives leading your company are leading the life of a celebrity, chances are they are not making decisions that will ensure long-term viability for you. Keep looking until you find a management team that clearly cares about their field.

CORPORATE OPPORTUNITIES

Through the years, I have heard from several top field leaders who want to trade in their upside for steady. In other words, they want to become corporate employees for direct selling companies and are willing to trade in the benefits of being a distributor. Here are the quick answers to the most frequently asked questions of those thinking about a corporate job:

- *How much can I earn?* Most former distributors enter corporations in regional sales manager positions which pay anywhere from $45k to $80k (a few may find pay up to $150K) depending on the amount of travel required and the size of the company. These positions typically have a bonus program that would be anywhere from 5-15% of the base salary.

- *Can I work from home?* Often you can work from home, but

typically the company will require you to travel to their headquarters at least once a quarter and many require you to travel throughout your region every week.

- *Where can I find opportunities?* There are a few search firms that specialize in direct selling that you will want to connect with. You can search the supplier portal of the Direct Selling Association website. I have also seen a list published on the Social Selling News website. You should also reach out to corporate executives you know, especially those who are working for a company different than the one you now sell for. On occasion companies will publish positions on their website. Most CEOs and founders, especially of small companies, are open to a cold call—especially if you have studied their company and have passion and enthusiasm for working for them.
- *Pros and cons*—The pros of working for a direct selling company are that you will have a steady and predictable paycheck and the chance to share what you have learned with others. Many regional sales representatives find it rewarding to help others succeed and they enjoy the chance to coach and speak and travel (often they attend company incentive trips).

    The cons of working for a company are that it is more difficult to significantly change your earnings and to measure the direct impact of the work you are doing. You're recognizing others more and often being recognized yourself less. And then there's corporate politics, which are real and can impact your career and job satisfaction significantly.

CHAPTER 18: THE DIRECT SELLING FRATERNITY—
Turning to Help from Other Direct Sellers

"When I started to get close to those who started and ran successful companies, I found a large group that truly wanted to help people achieve their dreams."

— PAUL ADAMS, CONSULTANT

N

So often I meet founders and executives of direct selling companies who are leading companies that are in trouble and who feel alone in the process. To these founders and executives my counsel is simple: "Ask other direct selling founders and executives for help." In all my years in this industry my outreach for help has only once been rebuffed and in that particular case it was due to the content of the material—that same CEO offered significant time and assistance just a few years later when I brought a founder to meet with him to discuss the company's challenges.

Unlike any professional group I'm aware of, direct selling executives act more like a fraternity than a group of competitors. Sure, there is competition and when given the chance, acts of aggressive business designed to win in a category. But for the most part this is an industry with an abundance mentality. Perhaps those leading direct selling companies understand that we still make up such a small percentage of the total retail opportunity that the goal is to help everyone succeed, knowing that a strong tide lifts all boats.

No matter what stage your company is in along the direct selling business lifecycle I've outlined in this book, if you haven't started to build your network and establish mutually beneficial relationships within the channel, now is the time. Here is what I urge all founders and CEOs of direct selling companies to do:

1. *Attend Direct Selling Events*—Start by joining and attending the Direct Selling Association events, particularly the annual meeting held every June and the marketing and communications session in December. The DSA also sponsors "Companies in Focus" which are smaller events that give executives a chance to tour the facilities of other direct selling companies and to listen to insight from their executives. If you are a female executive, don't miss the fall Women's Conference. I'm told it is filled with extraordinary conversation and is a place where deep and lasting relationships are formed and nourished.

    SUCCESS Partners holds a not-to-be-missed session every spring called "SUCCESS Partners University" with an agenda full of fast-moving content delivered from the industry's most successful CEOs and presidents, with a sprinkling of outstanding speakers and thought leaders. If your company is lucky enough to have $250 million or more in sales, seek an invitation to the exclusive "By Invitation Only" CEO Summit sponsored every fall in Southern California by SUCCESS Partners' Founder and CEO Stuart Johnson.

2. *Ask Other Executives for Help*—Even if you have not yet made friends and don't have deep relationships in the industry, ask for help from companies that have gone through similar situations or from executives you have come to admire—even if it's only from afar. Most of the executives in this channel will set aside competitive issues, keep your confidence and offer wise and caring advice and support.

3. *Paid Consultants*—There are dozens of experienced consultants in direct selling, most with previous executive experience of their own and all with experience helping companies in similar circumstances. Most of the consultants have areas of expertise such as customer service, start-ups, marketing and social media,

and compensation plans. A few are strong strategic consultants and several have been CEOs, some for more than one direct selling company.

While a few of the large strategy consulting companies have meaningful direct selling projects both on the strategy and IT sides of their practices, there are many individuals and mid-level consulting groups that will assure you they can help you despite their lack of experience in the industry. You will recall the story I shared in a previous chapter about Longaberger's failure. As I interviewed former executives from Longaberger, most of them pointed to the change in the company's compensation plan as the "point of no return." They were not so much critical of the decision to change the compensation, but of the fact that the plan was changed with the assistance of a consultant no one had heard of and who had little experience with proper implementation. The consultant's inexperience was evidenced by the lack of a process for selling the new program to either the corporate staff or the field. Anyone with prior involvement in compensation plan changes would have known that the buy-in is often more important than the contents of the change. That's why I recommend always making sure that any consultant you are considering comes with solid industry experience under their belt.

Ask others for referrals and search the DSA.org supplier site for help. Experienced direct selling vendors can refer you to others, too. Speaking of vendors...

4. *Engage Your Vendors*—One of the industry's most successful companies in the past 10 years was founded by someone who previously was a vendor to other direct selling companies. You may be surprised by how much help you can get from the IT, payment and other experienced direct selling vendors you have hired to provide services for your company. Oftentimes they

can offer general guidance, and more often they can connect you with other executives or consultants who can assist you with specific issues you are facing.

While I strongly believe that some experts will be more helpful than others, making sure you have someone you trust as a partner through the process of Renewal will make all the difference. Having been through this process on multiple occasions, both as an operating executive and as a consultant guiding others, I know that there will be moments when you think you are wasting money or time working with someone else. There will be times when both of you are convinced that the consultant/partner is no longer needed, and then a week later she'll offer insight that helps you overcome a new challenge and you'll be so grateful you still have her on your team.

In Closing...

Please visit my website, www.sidefactor.com, for resources and tools to guide you through every stage of your next Renewal. Feel free to reach out to me for help via email at brett@sidefactor.com. And if you are running a company or a sales organization that has successfully passed through the Shake-Out stage and found Renewal, I'd like to hear your story and learn from it. Please send me a message and share with me what you found helpful, what I didn't cover that worked for you, and what you learned along the way. With the permission of company founders, I will share stories and additional tips online as I receive them, so visit my website often for updates.

More companies can and must find their way to renewed growth and I hope you will be better prepared to lead your direct selling turnaround as a result of the thoughts and ideas you've learned here.

Whatever your results, I wish you all the best.

Be Happy!
B2

ACKNOWLEDGMENTS

I wish to acknowledge and express my gratitude for the dozens of executives, consultants and friends who have contributed content to this book. The direct selling industry is unique in the warm relationships executives have with one another and I have been blessed with many close friends.

I'm especially grateful for Milan Jensen, CEO and founder of Womenkind, for helping me lead a discussion on Renewal with several bright and accomplished executives.

Thank you to my editor Pamela Suarez, for her amazing work and skill in helping me improve my finished product considerably. I'm honored that Stuart Johnson, CEO of SUCCESS Partners agreed to help publish the book and appreciate the work of Todd Eliason, Patricia White, Julio Garcia, Megan Knoebel, Virginia Le, Pete Tepp, Terrie Bayless and Kristin Pfeil who helped me put meaningful finishing touches on the book prior to printing.

Finally, a special thanks for the love, support and patience of my wife and eternal companion, Erin, whom I love, and our children: Spencer and his wife Maris (the parents of our first grandson, Brooks, born while I was writing this book), Madison, Allison, Sydney and Kate, and to my father and friend Dr. Leon H. Blake.

ABOUT THE AUTHOR

Brett A. Blake is a direct selling veteran having led four companies (both person-to-person and party plan), served as a marketing executive for two others and served on several boards. He has served as the president, CEO or GM of seven companies, both public and private. The author of *Private Equity Investing in Direct Selling: Identifying Risks & Rewards*, Brett is a strategy consultant for direct selling companies and has been hired to advise investors on nearly a dozen direct selling transactions. He is one of the most experienced turnaround executives in direct selling, having led turnaround efforts at five companies. Brett is a personal advisor and coach to CEOs, boards and investors.

In addition to writing and speaking, Brett enjoys mountain biking and spending time with his wife Erin, their six children (one by marriage) and their newborn grandson. Brett will leave his consulting and speaking work beginning in July 2020, because he, Erin and their youngest daughter Kate have been called to lead a mission for the Church of Jesus Christ of Latter-day Saints for three years.